STRIKING IMPRESSIONS

A Visual Guide to Collecting U.S. Coins

By Robert R. Van Ryzin

Published by

**krause
publications**

700 East State St.   Iola WI 54990

Library of Congress Catalog Number: 91-75366
ISBN: 0-87341-176-5
Printed in the United State of America

CONTENTS

Introduction 5
U.S. Mint 6
The Minting Process 8
Half Cents 11
Large Cents 15
Large Cent Striking Impressions 20
Small Cents 25
Small Cent Striking Impressions 31
Two-Cent 45
Two-Cent Striking Impressions 46
Silver Three-Cent 47
Nickel Three-Cent 49
Half-Dimes 50
Half-Dime Striking Impressions 55
Nickel Five-Cent 56
Nickel Five-Cent Striking Impressions 60
Dimes 70
Dime Striking Impressions 78
20-Cent 85
20-Cent Striking Impressions 86
Quarters 87
Quarter Striking Impressions 97
Half Dollars 105
Half Dollar Striking Impressions 118
Silver Dollars 125
Silver Dollar Striking Impressions 132
Clad Dollars 140
Clad Dollar Striking Impressions 142
Gold Dollars 146
Gold Dollar Striking Impressions 148
Gold $2.50 149
Gold $2.50 Striking Impressions 153
Gold $3 156
Gold $3 Striking Impressions 157
Gold $4 158
Gold $5 159
Gold $10 164
Gold $20 168
Gold $20 Striking Impressions 172
Glossary 176
Glossary Striking Impressions 182
Bibliography 201
Silver Values 203
Gold Values 204

Introduction

From the moment a new collector is first drawn by the allure of U.S. coins — be it a worn-down, barely legible Indian Head nickel or a pristine new Lincoln cent — the quest for knowledge begins. How many were struck? How many survive? Does the coin have a collector value? Is it unusual to find such a coin in this condition?

A host of questions quickly come to mind.

The neophyte collector then enters a world of confusing terms, fanciful names and off-beat denominations. The insatiable desire for knowledge has begun.

Terms such as "exerque," "mule," and "die crack" are thrust at the collector with little or no explanation. Visualization is often left to the imagination.

But for the collector eager to learn how to distinguish one variety from another, or just wanting a ready reference to which to refer, it is the ability to clearly see what is meant that is most important. The cliche "a picture is worth a thousand words" certainly applies when it comes to numismatics.

That was the concept behind "Striking Impressions," first introduced in the Jan. 24, 1989, issue of Krause Publications' flagship publication, *Numismatic News*. By making use of Krause Publications' extensive photographic library and, when possible, enlarging photographs to present the key details, "Striking Impressions" came to life.

Some columns focus on the basics and terminology. Others are more in-depth, telling and, more importantly, clearly showing a method of distinguishing the genuine from the altered or one variety from another.

All are presented as a guide to the rich and enchanting world of collecting U.S. coins — a genuine effort to ease the collector into the world of collecting U.S. coins, and to present a taste, a glimmer, of what can be learned from further study.

Above all, this work — which features more than 90 of the original columns — is the product of an undying affection for what was once thought of as "the hobby of the kings," but is now the hobby of many.

— Robert R. Van Ryzin

Frank H. Stewart, who in the early 20th century purchased the site of the first Philadelphia Mint, commissioned this painting, "Ye Olde Mint," by Edwin Lamazure, showing the Mint as it would have appeared in late 18th century.

The U.S. Mint

Over the past 200 years there have been eight different mints in the United States, which variously served to assay, refine and alloy precious metals and, in the end, to strike coins.

Congress authorized the establishment of a mint in 1792 to be located in Philadelphia. A mint continues to operate in that city to this day.

Gold and silver discoveries and the expansion of trade and areas of settlement caused Congress to set up minting facilities in other cities. Three mints were built in 1838.

Those in Charlotte, N.C., and Dahlonega, Ga., struck gold coins from local mining output. Another, in New Orleans, was established to strike a wider range of coinage. Charlotte and Dahlonega were closed by the Civil War in 1861 and never reopened. The New Orleans Mint survived the war and continued to function afterward until 1909.

Following the discovery of the gold in California, a mint was established in San Francisco in 1854, which struck gold, silver and copper coins. This facility lost its mint status in 1955 and regained it in 1988. It currently strikes most of the U.S. proof coinage.

Carson City, Nev., located a short distance from Nevada's famous Comstock Lode (which provided much of its ore), was home to a mint that struck

In all, there have been seven branch facilities of the U.S. Mint. Only Denver, San Francisco and West Point remain in operation. Above is the earliest picture of the famed Carson City Mint, taken in June 1870. This branch struck silver coins bearing a distinctive "CC" mintmark.

silver coins from 1870 to 1893.

Further expansion came in 1906 when a mint was established in Denver, which has since become a primary manufacturer of U.S. coins.

The most recent addition to the mint lineup came in 1988 when what had been a bullion depository at West Point, in New York, was upgraded. This recognized the fact that coins had been struck there since the 1970s.

Mintmarks began appearing on U.S. coins following the opening of the branch facilities in the 1830s. The various mintmarks are listed below.

C — Charlotte
CC — Carson City
D — Dahlonega
D — Denver (no overlap with Dahlonega)
O — New Orleans
P — Philadelphia — This mintmark has been used only from 1942-1945 on nickels, on 1979 Anthony dollars and since 1980 on all other denominations except the cent. Traditionally, no mintmark meant the coin was produced in Philadelphia.
S — San Francisco
W — West Point

Coining processes continue to evolve. In earliest times striking was done by use of a hammer and a die. By the opening of the Philadelphia Mint in 1792 a screw press had come into use.

The minting process

In the simplest terms, striking of a coin involves a press, two dies, and a round metallic "planchet," cut from a strip of refined and rolled coinage metal. The press is constructed in such a way as to bring the two dies together under great pressure with the planchet between. One die has the obverse design and the other the reverse.

The designs on the dies are recessed and are a mirror or negative image of what, if all goes right, the final coin will look like. When the two dies come together the metal in the planchet is forced by the great pressure to flow up into the recessed areas of the die. The image is transferred as the metal actually flows into the cavities of the coinage die.

In the early days of the U.S. Mint, the press operation was quited simple: A hand-operated screw press would strike planchets as each was fed in by hand. Steam power improved the process in the 1830s, and refinements continue to the present time.

Currently, a press can contain two or four pairs of dies. Planchets are automatically fed to each die pair, and the striking process occurs simultaneously, with some presses capable of striking up to 750 coins per minute.

This 12-ton press was brought to the Carson City Mint in 1869, where it served throughout that Mint's tenure before being shipped to Philadelphia in 1899. It was subsequently used in Philadelphia, San Francisco and, in the 1960s, in Denver. Today, it is displayed at the Nevada State Museum (formerly the Carson City Mint), where it is occasionally used to strike medals.

Half cents

Liberty Cap (1793-1797)

Head facing left (1793)

Designer: Adam Eckfeldt. **Size:** 22 millimeters. **Weight:** 6.74 grams. **Composition:** 100-percent copper.

First Secretary of the Treasury Alexander Hamilton is largely to credit for the introduction of the nation's smallest denomination coin - the half cent. Hamilton proposed the denomination in his 1791 "Report on the Establishment of a Mint," claiming that it would aid the poor by allowing merchants to lower prices. Unfortunately, this never happened and the coin was largely considered a nuisance.

This first issue, struck on a thick planchet, is a one-year type, showing Liberty facing left and a Phrygian or "liberty" cap on pole. Its edge carried the lettering "Two Hundred for a Dollar."

The design is generally credited Adam Eckfeldt, a Mint assistant coiner who would later become chief coiner, and is thought to be largely patterned after the 1782 Libertas Americana medal by Augustin Dupre of France.

Although more than 35,000 of the 1793 Liberty Cap half cents were issued, it is scarce in all grades and, due to the high relief of the obverse design, is often found with weakly struck reverse details.

Head facing right (1794-1797)

Designers: Robert Scot (1794) and John Smith Gardner (1795). **Size:** 23.5 millimeters. **Weight:** 6.74 grams (1794-1795) and 5.44 grams (1795-1797). **Composition:** 100-percent copper.
Notes: Lettered-edge varieties of this type have "Two Hundred for a Dollar" inscribed around the edge. "Punctuated date" varieties have a comma after the "1" in the date. A 1797 "1 above 1" variety has a second "1" above the "1" in the date.

Redesigned by Mint engraver Robert Scot, the half cent would display Liberty facing to the right beginning in 1794, with Phrygian cap on pole. The former beaded border would give way to a serrated border. A modification of Scot's design, credited to John Smith Gardner, would show a smaller head on the coins from 1795-1797.

The first pieces of this type bore the edge lettering "Two Hundred for a Dollar," which was subsequently dropped. Due to increasing prices of copper the weight of the half cent was lowered in 1795 from 6.74 for the so-called thick-planchet coinage to 5.44 grams for the thin-planchet strikes.

This type includes a number of famous varieties, such as the 1795 and 1796 "no pole" coins, the former believed to have been the result of a regrinding of the die, and the latter, simply a mistake. [1] Both are rarities.

The increasing price and inadequate supply of copper also caused the Mint to turn to overstriking privately issued tokens or cutdown spoiled cents. The 1795 and 1797-dated half cents are sometimes found struck over tokens issued in 1794 and 1795 by the New York firm of Talbot, Allum & Lee.

Draped Bust (1800-1808)

Designer: Robert Scot. **Size:** 23.5 millimeters. **Weight:** 5.44 grams. **Composition:** 100-percent copper.
Notes: The wreath on the reverse was redesigned slightly in 1802, resulting in "reverse of 1800" and "reverse of 1802" varieties. The 1804 "stems" varieties have stems extending from the wreath above and on both sides of the fraction on the reverse. On the 1804 "crosslet 4" variety, a serif appears at the far right of the crossbar on the "4" in the date. Varieties of the 1805 strikes are distinguished by the size of the "5" in the date. Varieties of the 1806 strikes are distinguished by the size of the "6" in the date.

No half cents were coined dated 1798 or 1799. Featured beginning with the 1800-dated coinage of half cents was the Draped Bust design by Robert Scot, which had been introduced in 1795 on the silver dollar.

Much of the coinage of this type, including the 1800-dated pieces and all of the 1802-dated half cents, was struck on cutdown spoiled cent planchets. [2]

Varieties were the rule and not the exception. The 1804, for example, comes in "plain 4," "crosslet 4," "stemless wreath" and "stems to wreath" varieties.

Perhaps the most famous is the 1804 "Spiked Chin" variety, which gained its name from an additional thorn-like spike protruding from Liberty's chin, probably the result of accidental slip of the engraver's tool.

Classic Head (1809-1836)

Designer: John Reich. **Size:** 23.5 millimeters. **Weight:** 5.44 grams. **Composition:** 100-percent copper.

In 1807, John Reich was hired as assistant engraver to Robert Scot and began a redesign the nation's coinage. His "Classic Head" design of Liberty appeared on the cent in 1808 and on the half cent beginning in 1809.

Mintage of the half cent was halted after 1811 and would not resume until 1825.

The 1811 half cent, of which some 63,140 were struck, is considered scarce in all grades and a true rarity in uncirculated. Even rarer is an unofficial restrike of 1811 half cent using a reverse of 1802, apparently struck in the late 1850s. A dozen or so are thought to exist. [3]

Coinage would again be halted after 1829 and would not resume until 1831, with a design modified by chief engraver William Kneass and a raised rim created by the introduction of new equipment.

The 1831 is another rarity, with most known specimens in proof. [4] Restrikes were made in the late 1850s in "large berries" and "small berries" varieties.

The 1836 coinage is known only in proof, with restrikes having been made in the late 1850s.

Braided Hair (1840-1857)

Designer: Christian Gobrecht. **Size:** 23 millimeters. **Weight:** 5.44 grams. **Composition:** 100-percent copper.

Coinage of half cents from 1840-1848 would be in proof only, with no coins released for circulation. Modifications to the design are credited to Christian Gobrecht, who joined the Mint's service in 1836 as an engraver.

All of these dates are rare and all were restruck in the late 1850s. Coinage for circulation did not begin again until 1849 and would continue through 1857.

No coins were struck for circulation in 1852, although a Mint-produced restrike in proof exists.

Large cents

Flowing Hair (1793)

Chain reverse (1793)

Designer: Henry Voigt. **Size:** 26-27 millimeters. **Weight:** 13.48 grams. **Composition:** 100-percent copper.

Significantly larger than cents found in circulation today, the large cent (as it is now known) was first coined in 1793 in two major varieties, both of which featured a chain of 13 links on the reverse. One displays the word "America" completely; the other gives only "Ameri."

The design, by Henry Voigt, brought the Mint immediate criticism as some suggested that the chain - which was meant to be emblematic of the unity of the original 13 states - was a bad omen for liberty. The rather frightened portrayal of Liberty on the obverse was also subject to comment. [1]

The edge displayed a vine-and-bars decoration. Both varieties are generally found only in low grade and struck on poor copper.

Wreath reverse (1793)

Designer: Adam Eckfeldt. **Size:** 26-28 millimeters. **Weight:** 13.48 grams. **Composition:** 100-percent copper.

Criticism of the chain reverse appearing on the first U.S. large cent was likely the cause of the introduction of a new design with a remodeled Liberty and wreath on the reverse. All had a raised rim to protect the design and either a vine-and-bars design on the edge or the lettering, "One Hundred for a Dollar."

A great rarity of this type is the so-called "strawberry leaf" variety, with a sprig between the date and Liberty unlike those found on other specimens. Only four are known.

Liberty Cap (1793-1796)

Designers: Joseph Wright (1793-1795) and John Smith Gardner (1795-1796). **Size:** 29 millimeters. **Weight:** 13.48 grams (1793-1795) and 10.89 grams (1795-1796).
Notes: The heavier pieces were struck on a thicker planchet. The Liberty design on the obverse was revised slightly in 1794, but the 1793 design was used on some 1794 strikes. A 1795 "lettered edge" variety has "One Hundred for a Dollar" and a leaf inscribed on the edge.

After changing the design twice in 1793, the Mint did it a third time with introduction of the Liberty Cap design by Joseph Wright. Wright would serve only a short time as Mint engraver, dying of yellow fever in that same year.

Believed to have been patterned after the Libertas Americana medal struck by France in honor of the American Revolution, this new design showed Liberty facing right with a Phrygian cap on a pole.

The 1794 date is especially popular among large-cent collectors due to the number of varieties that exist and the extreme difficulty of completing a set. One of the most famous is the 1794 "starred reverse" cent on which the engraver for some unknown reason placed 94 five-pointed stars between the denticles on the coin's reverse.

The 1795-dated cents comes in both lettered edge and plain edge, the latter having been struck on thinner planchets. The high cost of copper caused Congress to lower the standard weight of the large cent from 208 grains to 168 grains in that year.

Also generally included under this design type is a piece known to collectors as the "Jefferson Head" cent. This rarity was apparently struck outside of the Mint, but with Congressional authorization, by John Harper as a coinage proposal during a period in which the Mint was under regular attack for its expenditures. [2]

Draped Bust (1796-1807)

Designer: Robert Scot. **Size:** 29 millimeters. **Weight:** 10.98 grams. **Composition:** 100-percent copper.
Notes: An 1801 "3 errors" variety has the fraction on the reverse reading "1/000,' has only one stem extending from the wreath above and on both sides of the fraction on the reverse, and "United" in "United States of America" appears as "Iinited."

In 1796, in the wake of the design change implemented on the silver dollar the year prior, Robert Scot's Draped Bust design (modeled after a drawing by Gilbert Stuart) was introduced on the large cent.

The 1799 cent is a famous rarity, with many of the known examples struck on rough pitted planchets and in low grade. The 1804 is another rarity of this series, generally found in low grade and struck on porous planchets. Restrikes of this date are also known, having been produced in the late 1850s from original, discarded mint dies.

Classic Head (1808-1814)

Designer: John Reich. **Size:** 29 millimeters. **Weight:** 10.89 grams. **Composition:** 100-percent copper.

Assigned shortly after his hiring to improve the quality of the designs on U.S. coins, Mint engraver John Reich created a portrait of Liberty that with variations would eventually be used on other copper, silver, and gold denominations. Reich's depiction of Liberty is said to have brought criticism for his portrayal of his fat mistress on the coin in order to make her famous. [3]

A number of varieties and overdates highlight this design, with many dates struck on dark and porous planchets. No cents were minted in 1815 due to a shortage of copper.

Coronet (1816-1839)

Designer: Robert Scot. **Size:** 28-29 millimeters. **Weight:** 10.89 grams. **Composition:** 100-percent copper.
Notes: The 1817 strikes have either 13 or 15 stars on the obverse.

Robert Scot again redesigned the cent in 1816. A new, slimmer Liberty wearing a coronet with the word "Liberty" inscribed on it would appear on the obverse through 1839. Due to the notable Randall Hoard, a keg of large cents discovered following the Civil War in Georgia and eventually sold to John Randall, the dates of 1816-1820 are considered plentiful in uncirculated.

A number of minor varieties and overdates spice this type.

Braided Hair (1840-1857)

Designer: Christian Gobrecht. **Size:** 27.5 millimeters. **Weight:** 10.89 grams. **Composition:** 100-percent copper.
Notes: 1840 and 1842 strikes are known with both small and large dates, with little difference in value. 1855 and 1856 strikes are known with both slanting and upright "5s" in the date, with little difference in value. A slightly larger Liberty head and larger reverse lettering were used beginning in 1843. One 1843 variety uses the old obverse with the new reverse.

Redesign of the cent began in 1835 after the death of former chief engraver Robert Scot with a number of transitional designs and colorful varieties being the result. Examples include the 1839 strikes that came to be known to large-cent collectors under the sobriquets - Silly Head, Booby Head and Petite Head.

Christian Gobrecht, a bank-note engraver before entering the Mint's employ, is generally credited with Braided Hair design that came into use in 1839 and was used for the remainder of large-cent series.

Beside design varieties, the Braided Hair type includes a number of engraving blunders, generally credited to James B. Longacre, who succeeded Gobrecht in 1844 as chief engraver. The most dramatic are the 1844/81 and 1851/81 overdates.

Striking Impressions

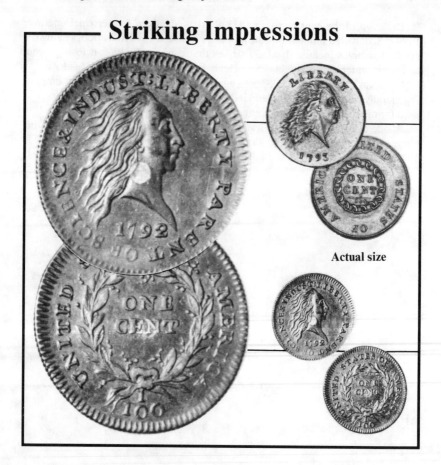

Actual size

1792
silver center
cent

Chief coiner Henry Voigt's plan was simple. He would put a little plug of silver in the center of the new U.S. cent and the problem of copper shortages would be lessened. The new coin could be smaller in size and thus use less copper and still have an intrinsic value of one cent. The copper would comprise three quarters of the cent's intrinsic value and the silver plug the remaining quarter. Voigt's plan was not accepted and today only about a dozen specimens are known. Also known are two planchets for the silver center cent discovered by Frank H. Stewart during the razing of the first Philadelphia Mint in 1907.

Striking Impressions

Federal issue

'Jefferson Head'
cent

1795 'Jefferson Head' cent

The year 1795 found the fledgling U.S. Mint in Philadelphia under attack from Congress for its high costs and delivery problems. It ultimately led to the introduction of contract coinage proposals, including one from John Harper, who struck a limited number of copper cents with a portrait that varied from that produced by the Mint. These rare specimens apparently gained the sobriquet among collectors as "Jefferson Head" from the resemblance of Liberty to Thomas Jefferson.

Striking Impressions

1803 reverse   1804 reverse

Diagnostic:
1804 large cent

The most common test in determining genuine 1804 large cents from those bearing altered dates is the positioning of the numeral "0" in the date on the coin's obverse and the letter "O" in "Of" on the reverse. On a genuine 1804 large cent those elements should be perfectly aligned. When a piece of paper is folded over the coin the edge of the paper should run directly through the center of the numeral "0" and the letter "O" on the opposite side. Don Taxay, in his *Counterfeit, Misstruck and Unofficial U.S. Coins*, provides an additional diagnostic. On the genuine 1804 large cent the second berry on the right extends below the right top vertical of the letter "E" in "One." Taxay notes that the 1804 cent bears a large 1/100th fraction found on only a few varieties of the 1803 cent. Such specimens, if altered to create an 1804 cent, would show the second berry in line with the right top vertical of the letter "E" in "One," rather than below it. Originals of the 1804 large cent were struck with normal die and a broken die (illustrated).

Striking Impressions

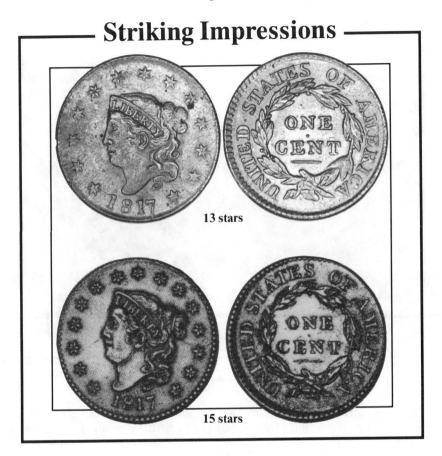

13 stars

15 stars

1817 large cent
'15 stars'

Was it simply a blunder that led to the creation of one of the more spectacular collectible varieties of the Scot "Coronet" large cents — the 1817 "15 stars" variety? No one seems to know for certain, but for some reason engraver Robert Scot placed 15 stars around the border of this variety rather than the standard 13 stars found on all other Matron Head large cents through 1835. Although considered rare in uncirculated, this popular variety (Newcomb-16) is available in lower grades.

Striking Impressions

Coin grading

Coin grading is at best a subjective art. Even with recent refinements to the grading scale, the introduction of third-party certified grading, and computerized grading, the debate over what makes a coin one level higher or lower on the grading scale still flares up between knowledgeable numismatists. Generally, it has been assumed that the person who owns a given coin has the tendency to judge it to be slightly better than the potential buyer — hoping to extract as much profit from the sale as possible. But if this is true, then Bangs, Merwin & Co. of New York deserved an award for conservative and wretchedly honest grading. For though many collectors would like their large cents to look as nice as the ones above, and coin sellers would certainly like to handle choice large cents, Bangs, Merwin & Co. used a unique marketing approach in its Dec. 17, 1869, sale of the J.M. Wilbur collection. According to Emmanuel Joseph Attinelli's *A Bibliography of American Numismatic Auction Catalogues 1828-1875*, reprinted in 1976 by Quarterman Publications Inc., this 1,958-lot auction featured some 60 large cents dated 1847 with the highest grade to any given as "barely fair," while others were described by the cataloger, Edward Cogan, as " 'poor,' 'poorer,' 'worse,' 'extremely poor,' 'unusually poor,' 'wretchedly poor,' 'still worse,' 'exceedingly poor,'" and " 'poorer still.' " Attinelli observed that "barely fair" was also the highest grade found on some 300 lots of the sale, "which were sold at one cent each, if the catalogue before me is correctly priced."

Small cents

Flying Eagle (1856-1858)

Designer: James B. Longacre. **Size:** 19 millimeters. **Weight:** 4.67 grams. **Composition:** 88-percent copper, 12-percent nickel.

Unpopular and costly to produce, the 27.5-millimeter large cent was abandoned in 1857 in favor of a small cent measuring only 19 millimeters. The new small cent, comprised of 88-percent copper and 12-percent nickel, was eagerly welcomed by the public.

Coinage for 1856 was in the form of a pattern issue that has since come to be largely accepted as part of the regular U.S. coinage series. This is likely due to the distribution of more than 600 1856 Flying Eagle cents to congressmen and others.[1] Restrikes were made in 1858 and 1859.

Coinage began in earnest in 1857 with the Mint accepting large cents and foreign silver in exchange for the new cent.

Mintage of the regular-issue Flying Eagle cent was high, with 17.45 million struck in 1857 and an additional 24.6 million minted in 1858. The 1858 issue includes large- and small-letters varieties.

Although the new small cent was popular with the public, the design and metallic composition led to striking problems and the Flying Eagle design was dropped after only two years of regular-issue coinage.

Indian Head (1859-1909)

Copper-nickel composition, laurel wreath (1859)

Designer: James B. Longacre. **Size:** 19 millimeters. **Weight:** 4.67 grams. **Composition:** 88-percent copper, 12-percent nickel.

First issues of the Indian Head cent, designed by James B. Longacre, displayed on the obverse Liberty wearing an Indian headdress. A laurel wreath is shown on the reverse. This wreath would be abandoned the following year in favor of an oak wreath. Mintage of this one-year type was 36.4 million.

Copper-nickel composition, oak wreath (1860-1864)

An oak wreath and shield design graced the reverse of the Indian Head cent for the remainder of its coinage, the change probably having been made due to problems with striking of the laurel-wreath reverse. [2] Mintages were high, with the peak year coming in 1863, with 49.84 million struck, and the low years being 1861 (10.1 million) and 1864 (13.74 million).

Bronze composition (1864-1909)

Weight: 3.11 grams. **Composition:** 95-percent copper, 5-percent tin and zinc.

Hoarding of the copper-nickel cents, as well as other precious-metal coins, during the Civil War, along with the short supply and difficulty of working with nickel, led the Mint to turn to a bronze composition for the cent. [3]

The new bronze cents were comprised of 95-percent copper and five-percent zinc and tin, and were thinner and lighter than the copper-nickel cents.

The first-year issue came with or without an "L" - representing the designer, James B. Longacre - located between the hair and lower feather of the Indian's headdress. The "with L" specimens command a premium. The 1873 date is known in both closed-3 and open-3 varieties.

A change in the design hub in 1886 also created two varieties. The first shows the final feather of the headdress pointing between the "IC" in "America." Those struck through the remainder of that year and the rest of the Indian Head series have the feather pointing between the "CA" of "America."

The series best-known rarity is the 1877, with a mintage of 852,500. It is often found weakly struck.

Branch-mint coinage of cents began in 1908 at the San Francisco Mint with the low-mintage 1908-S. The 1909-S is the lowest mintage regular-issue Indian Head cent (309,000 struck) and a premium coin in all grades.

Lincoln (1909 to date)

Wheat reverse, bronze composition (1909-1942)

Designer: Victor D. Brenner. **Size:** 19 millimeters. **Weight:** 3.11 grams. **Composition:** 95-percent copper, 5-percent tin and zinc.

The Lincoln cent, designed by Victor D. Brenner and released to commemorate the 100th anniversary of Abraham Lincoln's birth, holds the distinction of being the first regular-issue U.S. coin to bear the portrait of a U.S. president. The reverse design featured wheat stalks. With some minor modifications this design was used through 1958.

When released in 1909 the Lincoln cent bore Brenner's initials "V.D.B." at the bottom of the reverse. Public criticism of the prominent placement of the engraver's initials led to deletion of the "V.D.B." in that same year, and created one of coin collecting's most popular varieties, the 1909-S V.D.B. with a mintage of 484,000. Brenner's initials would not be restored again until 1918 and then only on the truncation of Lincoln's shoulder.

Other keys of this design type include the 1914-D, 1922 "plain" and the 1931-S. The 1922 "plain" is so termed because of a worn die, which caused some Denver Mint coins to appear without the appropriate "D" mintmark.

As no cents were struck at the Philadelphia Mint in that year, the 1922 "plain" became a popular variety. Many other dates are found weakly struck and elusive in high grade with full mint red.

Steel composition (1943)

Weight: 2.7 grams. **Composition:** steel coated with zinc.

In 1943 wartime demand for copper led to the introduction of a zinc-coated steel cent, which would be used until the following year. Many today are found corroded. Others have been reprocessed - the top layer of zinc stripped from the surface and replated - for sale to collectors.

Mintages on the 1943 zinc-coated steel cents were very high and examples are common. The 1943-S, with a mintage of 191.55 million, carries the highest premium of the three mints that struck the coins - Philadelphia, Denver, and San Francisco - though it is slight.

A very small number of 1943-dated cents struck on copper planchets were inadvertently minted and are great rarities. Unfortunately, in the years since its discovery a number of steel cents have been plated with copper by those hoping to pass the coins as copper cents. These can be detected by attraction to a magnet. On others, authentication is mandatory.

Copper-zinc composition (1944-1958)

Weight: 3.11 grams. **Composition:** 95-percent copper, 5-percent zinc.
Notes: The 1955 "doubled die" has distinct doubling of the date and lettering on the obverse.

Copper returned to the cent in 1944 in the form of metal salvaged from spent World War II shell casings. These were employed through 1946. The most famous variety of this type is the 1955 doubled die, which was the result of the use of an accidentally doubled obverse die.

Memorial reverse, bronze composition (1959-1962)

Reverse designer: Frank Gasparro. **Weight:** 3.11 grams.
Notes: The date was modified in 1960 resulting in large-date and small-date varieties.

In 1959 the wheat-ear reverse was abandoned in favor of a depiction of the Lincoln Memorial, a design meant to commemorate the 150th anniversary of Lincoln's birth.

This type includes two popular, but low premium, varieties that can still, occasionally, be found in circulation - the 1960 small- and large-date cents, struck at both the Denver and Philadelphia mints.

Brass composition (1962-1982)

Composition: 95-percent copper, 5-percent zinc.
Notes: The date was modified in 1970 and 1982 resulting in large-date and small-date varieties. A 1972 "doubled die" shows doubling of "In God We Trust."

In 1969 a limited number of cents were released from the San Francisco Mint with a doubled obverse, and in 1972 the Philadelphia Mint released a cent with a doubled obverse. Both exhibit wide doubling of the features.

Though of much lesser value, small- and large-date varieties of the 1970-S are also well known to collectors. The small-date variety is a premium coin. It can also be found on proof strikes.

Copper-plated zinc composition (1982 to date)

Weight: 2.5 grams. **Composition:** 97.6-percent zinc, 2.4 percent copper.
Notes: A 1983 "doubled die reverse" shows doubling of "United States of America." A 1984 "doubled die" shows doubling of Lincoln's ear on the obverse.

In 1982 the rising cost of copper led the Mint to turn to a copper-plated zinc composition, which has been in use ever since, although problems with discoloring hark back to the 1943 zinc-coated steel cents.

Striking Impressions

Second restrike

Original

Confederate cent

The Confederate States of America produced only two coins of its own during its short existence — a half dollar and a cent. Neither was placed in full production and the existence of both was kept a secret until well after the close of the war. In the case of the 1861 copper-nickel Confederate cent, its existence wasn't known until late in 1873 when Robert Lovett Jr., a Philadelphia engraver and die sinker, accidently spent one of the coins in a Philadelphia tavern. Learning of the missspent Confederate cent, Capt. John W. Haseltine was able to purchase that specimen and, after repeated visits to Lovett, secured the original dies and the remaining 11 Confederate cents. He also learned the story of the coin's creation. Apparently, Lovett had been approached by the Confederacy to produce dies for the coin. Lovett combined the obverse depiction of Liberty from one of his 1861 store cards with a new reverse. When the plan fell through, Lovett kept the existence of the coins a well-guarded secret until he accidentally disposed of the one that he had carried as a pocket piece. In 1874 Haseltine used the original dies to create restrikes in gold, silver and copper. The dies were again used in 1961 by Robert Bashlow to produce transfer dies from which restrikes were made in a variety of metals. By the time of Bashlow's restrikes, the dies had already been cancelled, therefore, examples of the second restrike are heavily ladened with chisel marks from the cancellation. Modern replicas of no real value also exist.

Striking Impressions

Flying Eagle cent

A combination of two previously used coinage designs, a new small cent, now termed the Flying Eagle cent, made its debut in 1856, sporting on the obverse an eagle modeled after that which appeared on the 1836-1839 Gobrecht dollar (based on drawings by Titian Peale). The reverse by James B. Longacre, who is credited with design of the Flying Eagle cent, shows the same wreath as appeared on the $3 gold coin beginning in 1854. Though many lined up at the Mint to exchange old large cents for new small cents, not everyone found joy in the design now popular among collectors. James C. Risk, in an article in the Vol. V, No. 2, 1964 issue of *Coin Review*, published by Stack's Rare Coins of New York, reported on the discovery by Stack's of a notebook kept by Longacre that included comments on the reception of the new cent. Some critics of the day complained that the new cents might be easily swallowed by children, while others took Longacre and the Mint to task for the portrayal of the eagle on the coin's obverse. One critic, quoted by Risk, said it resembled a table napkin or pen wiper. Risk wrote, "The Cent seemed to demonstrate what is really an old American characteristic best summed up in a recent comment by the present Attorney General of the United States when he said, 'One fifth of the poeple are against everything all the time." To which, might be added, the quote, "critics are people who come down from the mountain after the battle is over and shoot the dead." For his part, Longacre wrote in his notebook, which was subsequently donated by Stack's to the Smithsonian Institution, that the introduction of the cent had "given occasion to the numismatic critics great and small, for a pretty elaborate display of their abilities," and, while he defended the cent, made it clear that he did not select the eagle for the obverse of the coin, nor design it.

Striking Impressions

Diagnostic:
1856 Flying Eagle cent

A diagnostic of the 1856 Flying Eagle cent that can be used to distinguish genuine examples from those altered from an 1858 Flying Eagle cent is the "5" in the date. Genuine examples show a slanting "5," with the ball of the "5" extending behind the upright. The 1858 coins show the numeral "5" as vertical and the ball in line with the upright.

Striking Impressions

Large letters

Small letters

1858
Flying Eagle cent

Two distinct varieties were struck of the 1858 Flying Eagle cent, large letters and small letters. The varieties are most easily identified by viewing the "AM" in the word "America" on the coin's obverse. On the large-letter variety the legs of the "A" and "M" touch. On the small-letter variety there is a noticeable gap between the letters.

Striking Impressions

Without "L"

With "L"

1864 Indian Head cent with 'L'

In 1864 the letter "L," representing the coin's designer, James B. Longacre, was added to the bonnet ribbon of the bronze Indian Head cent. As production of the 1864 "L" cents began late in the year, mintages were lower than for the 1864 cent without the "L" — accounting for the higher value of the 1864 "L" variety. A simple means of identifying even a heavily worn 1864 "L" cent is to note the tip of the Indian's bust. On the coins that carry the "L" the tip of the bust is pointed. On the specimens without the "L" the tip of the bust is rounded.

Striking Impressions

Diagnostic:
1877
Indian Head cent

There are several keys to identifying a genuine 1877 circulation strike Indian Head cent. The most common reference point is on the reverse. As with other Indian Head cents from the period, genuine specimens will exhibit a characteristic weakness at the bottom right angle of the "N" in "One" and on the "E" in "Cent." Also note that in the date the second "7" extends below the first "7." Most counterfeits will display the 7s in line.

— Striking Impressions —

1909 V.D.B. Lincoln cent

Shortly after its release into circulation, complaints began filtering into the Mint concerning the prominent placement of designer Victor D. Brenner's initials on the reverse of the Lincoln cent. In reality, the initials were less prominent than "Brenner," which appeared in same position on the original models. No doubt use of the complete surname would have brought an even greater outcry, likened to what was heard when Christian Gobrecht's last name appeared above the date on the obverse of 1836 patterns of the Gobrecht dollar.

Striking Impressions

Genuine
1914-D

1914-D Lincoln cent

The 1914-D is one of the keys to the Lincoln cent series and as such has been subjected to all forms of counterfeiting and alteration in the years since its release. One of the more common alterations is from a 1944-D to a 1914-D. Such coins should be easy to spot as the removal of part of the "4" next to the "9" will leave a large gap between the "9" and the newly created "1." Also, any altered 1914-D made from a cent struck after 1918 will display Victor D. Brenner's initials on the shoulder truncation at the bottom of the bust of Lincoln or may show signs of removal. The initials did not appear on a genuine 1914-D, but were added to the Lincoln cent obverse in 1918.

Striking Impressions

1922 'plain'
Lincoln cent

Plugged and worn dies have generally been blamed as the culprits in the creation of the 1922 "plain" cent. The now defunct American Numismatic Association Certification at one time identified three separate dies used in the production of the Denver cents without mintmarks. Its finding appeared in the October 1984 issue of *The Numismatist* and are a valuable reference to this variety, which can also be found with portions of "D" still visible. Wide differences in premiums exist and confusion reigns regarding what constitutes a "plain" or "weak D" 1922 cent. Beware of counterfeits produced by removal of the mintmark from 1922-D cents. Authentication is recommended.

Striking Impressions

Doubled dies
1955 and 1972

Two of the most popular collectible doubled-die coins produced are those struck at the Philadelphia Mint in 1955 and 1972. Both carry significant premiums in all grades and were created from obverse dies that doubled in the transfer process from the working hub. Working dies are produced by several blows from a positive die known as a hub. In the case of the 1955 and 1972 doubled dies, at least one of the strikes of the obverse working hub to an obverse working die was shifted out of alignment. All coins produced from the mistruck die thus presented an obviously doubled obverse and a normal reverse.

Striking Impressions

1955
Doubled die

1955
"Poorman's Double Die"

1955
'Poorman's Double Die'

This relatively worthless variety gained notoriety after the release of the scarce doubled-die cent of 1955. The "Poorman's Double Die," as it was called, was promoted as a means of obtaining an inexpensive version of the popular 1955 doubled-die cent. The 1955 doubled die, which commands a hefty premium even in low grades, was created through an errant strike from a positive die, known as a hub, used to produced working dies. At least one of the blows from the hub was out of alignment, causing doubling in the working die. All coins struck from this die display this scarce form of prominent doubling. The "Poorman's Double Die," on the other hand, is nothing more than die polishing variety and, therefore, of little more than curiosity value.

Striking Impressions

Small date

Large date

Small- and large-date
1960 Lincoln cents

In 1960 a change in the master dies led to the creation of the small- and large-date Lincoln cents struck at the Philadelphia and Denver mints. The more valuable small-date cent variety can be distinguished from its large-date counterpart by the more compact appearance of the "6" and its shorter tail. Another diagnostic is that the top of the "1" on the small-date cent aligns with the top of the "9." The large-date variety also shows the numerals as being slightly closer together.

Striking Impressions

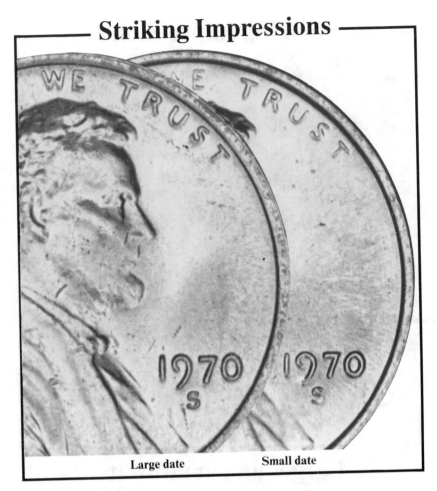

Large date   **Small date**

Small- and large-date
1970-S Lincoln cents

In 1970 a change in the master dies used to produce cents at the San Francisco Mint created a popular variety — the 1970-S small-date cent. The small-date cent can be most readily distinguished from its large-date counterpart by viewing the top part of the loop in the digit "9." On the large-date variety this loop curves at a 45-degree angle toward the leg of the "9." On the more valuable small-date variety this same loop turns more sharply in toward the body of the "9." The position of the "7" in the date can also be used to distinguish the varieties. On the large-date cent the "7" appears to rest just below the remaining three digits in the date. On the small-date cent the tops of all four digits are in line.

—— Striking Impressions ——

| Small date | Large date |

Large- and small-date
1982 Lincoln cent

The year 1982 was one of change for the Lincoln cent. The former brass composition was dropped in favor of copper-plated zinc. In that same year modification of the coinage dies led to the creation of the so-called 1982 small-date cent. Circulation coinage at West Point, Denver and proofs struck in San Francisco were of the old large-date dies. Philadelphia began coinage with the large-date dies before switching to the new small-date dies in September 1982. It would strike both the brass and the copper-plated zinc composition cents with both the old (large-date) dies and the new (small-date) dies. The small-date die featured letters and date with strongly beveled edges and a slightly lower relief to Lincoln's bust. The "8" in the date was also repositioned and on the small-date variety appears more in line with the other numerals. The upper loop of the "8" is also noticeably smaller than the lower loop.

Two-cent

(1864-1873)

Designer: James B. Longacre. **Size:** 23 millimeters. **Weight:** 6.22 grams. **Composition:** 95-percent copper, 5-percent tin and zinc.

The suspension of specie payments in the early 1860s and the outbreak of the Civil War led to the hoarding of all precious metals, including the copper-nickel cent, the composition of which was changed to bronze in 1864. Mint Director James Pollock believed that the introduction of a two-cent piece, also of bronze, would be of convenience to the public.

Unfortunately, the public found little use for the new denomination. After opening mintages in the range of 20 million per year, production of the two-cent piece dropped to a scant 65,000 in 1872, the last year of coinage for circulation.

A small number of proofs were made the following year for the benefit of collectors before the denomination was officially dropped by the Coinage Act of 1873.

The two-cent piece holds the distinction of being the first regular-issue U.S. coin to bear the motto "In God We Trust," which would eventually come into standard use.

The 1864 strike is found in small- and large-motto varieties.

—— Striking Impressions ——

Small motto

Large motto

Small- and large-motto
1864 two-cent pieces

In 1864 the religious motto "In God We Trust" made its first appearance on the newly introduced two-cent piece. Two varieties of the motto exist on the coins of 1864, with the small-motto variety being the scarcest and most valuable. Several methods exist for easily identifying the small- and large-motto coins. On the small-motto variety the inside space in the letters "O" and "D" of "God" is wide and round. On the large-motto variety it is narrow and oval. Another helpful reference point is the first "T" in the word "Trust." On the small-motto variety the "T" touches the ribbon fold at its left. It does not touch the ribbon fold on the large-motto variety. Also, on the small-motto coin a stem can be seen on the leaf appearing below the word "Trust." The stem is absent from the large-motto variety.

Silver three-cent

Type I (1851-1853)

Designer: James B. Longacre. **Size:** 14 millimeters. **Weight:** .8 grams. **Composition:** 75-percent silver (.0193 ounces), 25-percent copper.

The smallest U.S. silver coin by diameter, the silver three-cent piece, which measured only 14 millimeters, was authorized in 1851 by an act of Congress as a convenient denomination with which to purchase newly issued three-cent postage stamps.

The first design type, struck from 1851-1853, has a six-pointed star on the obverse with no lines bordering. Unlike other silver coins, which were issued in a standard of 90-percent silver and 10-percent copper, the Type I silver three-cent pieces were minted in 75-percent silver and 25-percent copper.

This type included the only branch-mint coinage of the silver three-cent piece, with 720,000 struck in 1851 at the mint in New Orleans. It is also the scarcest date.

Type II (1854-1858)

Weight: .75 grams. **Composition:** 90-percent silver (.0218 ounces), 10-percent copper.

In 1854 the design was changed to feature three lines bordering the star on the obverse. An olive sprig and arrows were added to the reverse.

These, and subsequent silver three-cent pieces, would conform with higher denomination silver coins by reducing the copper alloy from 25 percent to 10 percent. The weight was lowered from .80 grams to .75 grams.

Type II silver three-cent pieces are generally found weakly struck.

Type III (1859-1873)

In 1859 the design was again changed, probably due to the striking problems of the previous two designs, which particularly affected the Type II coinage. The Type III coins would have only two lines bordering the star.

At first mintages of the silver three-cent pieces were high, with the peak being 18,663,500 in 1852. But by the 1860s, in the wake of the suspension of specie payments and the Civil War, mintages began to fall off, as all precious metals were hoarded.

After 1862 coinage of the silver three-cent piece plummeted to a low in 1872 when only 1,950 were struck. During the final year of coinage, only proofs were minted.

Nickel three-cent

(1865-1889)

Designer: James B. Longacre. **Size:** 17.9 millimeters. **Weight:** 1.94 grams. **Composition:** 75-percent copper, 25-percent nickel.

Composed of 75-percent copper and 25-percent nickel, but with a silvery appearance, the nickel three-cent piece was released in 1865 largely to get rid of the disliked three-cent fractional paper notes authorized in 1863, many of which had become ragged and torn. The nickel three-cent coins were paid out in exchange for redemption of the paper notes.

The first-year mintage was a high 11.382 million, but afterwards mintages began to drop - the dates from 1884-1887 being especially low mintage and carrying strong premiums in all grades. Only proofs were struck in 1877-1878 and in 1886.

The high percentage of nickel used in the composition caused striking problems, leading many dates in this series to be found weakly struck.

Half dimes

Flowing Hair (1794-1795)

Designer: Robert Scot. **Size:** 16.5 millimeters. **Weight:** 1.35 grams. **Composition:** 89.24-percent silver (.0388 ounces), 10.76-percent copper.

Mint engraver Robert Scot's depiction of Liberty facing right and a small eagle within a wreath appeared on the first half dimes struck at the Mint. Combined mintage of both dates came to only 86,416, all of which were actually struck in 1795. Both dates are scarce and rare in uncirculated. Many varieties exist.

Draped Bust (1796-1805)

Small-eagle reverse (1796-1797)

Designer: Robert Scot. **Size:** 16.5 millimeters. **Weight:** 1.35 grams. **Composition:** 89.24-percent silver (.0388 ounces), 10.76-percent copper.
Notes: The 1797 strikes have either 13, 15 or 16 stars on the obverse.

Robert Scot's Draped Bust Liberty, modeled after an original drawing by famed artist Gilbert Stuart, began appearing on the half dime in 1796.

The most famous of a number of 1796 varieties is one in which the word "Liberty" appears as "Likerty," due to worn dies.

Heraldic-eagle reverse (1800-1805)

No half dimes were struck from 1798-1799 and by the time coinage resumed in 1800 the small-eagle reverse had been replaced by a heraldic eagle.

Like the 1796 coinage, a variety of the 1800 strikes displays the word "Liberty" as "Likerty," this time, however, a defective letter punch, not wear to the die, is thought to have been the problem.

The 1802 half dime is a famous U.S. rarity, with 3,060 thought to have been struck. Of the small number of specimens still in existence, most are in low grade and often weakly struck.

No half dimes were struck in 1804. Coinage resumed in 1805 with 15,600 half dimes minted.

Capped Bust (1829-1837)

Designer: William Kneass. **Size:** 15.5 millimeters. **Weight:** 1.35 grams. **Composition:** 89.24-percent silver (.0388 ounces), 10.76-percent copper.
Notes: Design modifications in 1835, 1836 and 1837 resulted in variety combinations with large and small dates, and large and small "5 C." inscriptions on the reverse.

Half dime coinage was stopped after the 1805 output and would not resume until 1829 with John Reich's Capped Bust design, which was already appearing on the other silver denominations.

This would be the first half dime to express the denomination, shown as "5 C." below the eagle on the reverse.

Seated Liberty (1837-1873)

No stars around rim (1837-1838)

Designer: Christian Gobrecht. **Size:** 15.5 millimeters. **Weight:** 1.34 grams. **Composition:** 90-percent silver (.0388 ounces), 10-percent copper.

In a move aimed at unifying coinage designs, Christian Gobrecht's Seated Liberty design was placed on the half dime in 1837. The design had first made its appearance in 1836 on the dollar.

The 1837 half dime is found in both small- and large-date varieties.

The 1838-O, the first branch-mint half dime, with a mintage of 70,000, is scarce and considered very rare in uncirculated.

Stars around rim (1838-1853)

Notes: Two varieties of 1838 are distinguished by the size of the stars on the obverse. An 1839-O with reverse of 1838-O variety was struck from rusted reverse dies. The result is a bumpy surface on this variety's reverse.

In 1838 13 stars were added to the obverse design of the half dime. Pieces from 1837-1840 lack drapery from Liberty's left elbow, which was added in 1840, in remodeling of the design by Robert Ball Hughes.

The 1840 half dime is known in "no drapery" and "drapery" versions, struck by both the Philadelphia and New Orleans mints. The drapery varieties of that date had lower mintages and bring higher premiums.

Other varieties include the 1848 medium- and large-date coins and the 1849 with overdates of 9/6 and 9/8.

The 1846, of which 27,000 were coined, is a premium key in all grades. Also very scarce is the 1853-0 without arrows at date.

Arrows at date (1853-1855)

Weight: 1.24 grams. **Composition:** 90-percent silver (.0362 ounces), 10-percent copper.

The discovery of gold in California in 1848 drove the price of silver up. In the process, silver coins began to disappear from circulation as bullion value exceeded face value. Those that weren't melted were simply hoarded.

Attempting to rectify the problem, the Mint Act of 1853 reduced the weight of all silver coins, with the exception of the silver dollar, to fall in line with a subsidiary dollar of 384 grains.

First-year mintage at Philadelphia of the reduced-weight half dime was 13.210 million. The low-mintage date is the 1855-0, of which 600,000 were struck.

Arrows at date removed (1856-1859)

In 1856 the arrows were dropped from the date area, although the weight of the half dime remained at the new, lower level.

A famous variety is the 1858 over inverted date, a Mint blunder generally credited to the hand of chief engraver James B. Longacre, who during his tenure made a number of such mistakes.

Obverse legend (1860-1873)

In 1860 the legend "United States of America" replaced stars on the obverse of the half dime. A new wreath design was employed for the reverse.

Philadelphia strikes from 1863-1867 are all low mintage and scarce in all grades.

The 1870-S half dime is a classic rarity. No specimens were known to exist until 1978 when one was discovered in a dealer's junk box and brought to the attention of the collecting public in an article in the Sept. 9, 1978, issue of *Numismatic News*.

Although coinage of the silver half dime continued through 1873, the coin had become unpopular. The introduction and public acceptance of the Shield five-cent piece, comprised of 75-percent copper and 25-percent nickel, along with problems of keeping silver in circulation led to the elimination of the half dime when mint laws were revised by the Coinage Act of 1873.

Striking Impressions

1792 half disme

One of the most romantic of all U.S. coins is the 1792 half disme, believed to have been minted from silver deposited by George Washington. The initial coinage of half dimes (then known as a half disme) is thought to have been struck in the cellar of property owned by John Harper at Sixth and Cherry Streets, as the new mint site had not yet been acquired. In all, 1,500 1792 half dismes are believed to have been struck, many of which were given out as souvenirs and placed into circulation. In his November 6, 1792, address Washington optimistically reported, "There has been a small beginning in the coinage of half dismes; the want of small coins in circulation calling the first attention to them." Coinage of the half dime would not, however, begin on any scale until 1794.

Nickel five-cent

Shield (1866-1883)

Designer: James B. Longacre. **Size:** 20.5 millimeters. **Weight:** 5 grams. **Composition:** 75-percent copper, 25-percent nickel.

Much like the nickel three-cent piece, which was introduced in 1865 to redeem three-cent fractional paper notes, the nation's first base-metal five-cent piece was suggested by Mint Director James Pollock, in that same year, as a substitute for five-cent fractional notes.

The federally issued Fractional Currency notes were one of a number of war-time substitutes for scarce precious-metal coinage. After the war the notes continued to circulate, even though the worn and tattered paper money was largely disliked by the public.

The first issues of the five-cent piece showed rays between the stars on coins struck in 1866 and a portion of the 1867 coinage.

Striking problems with the "with rays" design evidently led to its replacement in 1867, but not before some 2.019 million of the 1867 "with rays" coins were struck. Mintage of the "no rays" variety far exceeded that of its predecessor, reaching 28.89 million, making the "with rays" variety a scarce and popular coin.

Unlike the three-cent piece, the nickel as it came to be generally known, was readily accepted and continues to be a useful part of the nation's coinage system. Other notable dates of this type include the 1871, with a mintage of 561,000; the 1873 "closed 3" variety; and the 1879-1881 dates, all of which sported low mintages. No five-cent pieces were struck for circulation in 1877 and 1878.

Liberty (1883-1913)

Designer: Charles E. Barber. **Size:** 21.2 millimeters. **Weight:** 5 grams. **Composition:** 75-percent copper, 25-percent nickel.

Designed by Mint engraver Charles Barber, the first Liberty Head nickels bore only a Roman numeral "V" within a wreath and failed to include the word "cents." The design flaw was soon noted by the unscrupulous, who found the five-cent piece's similarity in size to the half eagle made it ready prey for gold-plating so that it could be passed at the higher value.

Some 5.479 million 1883-dated "centless" coins were struck before the design was changed to feature the word "cents" below the wreath.

Among the high premium dates are the 1885, 1886 and 1912-S.

The most famous coin in the series is the 1913 Liberty Head nickel, which was clandestinely struck by a Mint employee after the order to change to new Indian Head nickel design had already been received. Only five 1913 Liberty Head nickels are thought to exist, all of which are proofs.

Indian Head (1913-1938)

Designer: James Earle Fraser. **Size:** 21.2 millimeters. **Weight:** 5 grams. **Composition:** 75-percent copper, 25-percent nickel.

Popularly termed the Buffalo nickel, after the reverse depiction (which is actually a bison and not a buffalo), the Indian Head nickel is the product of an era of coinage redesign inspired by President Theodore Roosevelt.

The obverse bore a composite portrait of a Plains Indian prepared by Fraser from various models. Numismatic tradition names the models as Iron Tail, a Sioux; Two Moons, a Cheyenne; and John Big Tree, an Iroquois.

Research by this author has shown, however, that John Big Tree - even though he took great pride in claiming credit and in the 1960s was employed by Falstaff Brewery as the Indian Head nickel model - was merely an actor. [1]

The more likely third model was Adoeette, a Kiowa, who was known as Chief Big Tree.

First examples of the Indian Head nickel showed the bison on a raised mound. The design was found to wear quickly and was replaced that same year to place the denomination in recess and protect it from wear.

Even this change could not escape the fact that the entire design, although aesthetically pleasing, was in too high relief for high-speed coinage. Many dates are, therefore, found weakly struck. This is particularly noticeable on the coinage of Denver and San Francisco. The 1926-D is notorious in this regard.

This type includes one of the 20th century's most famous overdates, the 1918/7-D, and a 1916 nickel with doubled obverse. Also sought after is the 1937-D "three-legged" Indian Head nickel, which, due to excessive regrinding of a damaged die, lacks part of the left front foreleg of the bison.

An interesting overmintmark, the 1938-D/S apparently occurred when planned coinage at the San Francisco Mint did not occur and a previously prepared die was pressed into service.

Jefferson (1938 to date)

Prewar composition (1938-1942)

Designer: Felix Schlag. Size: 21.2 millimeters. Weight: 5 grams. Composition: 75-percent copper, 25-percent nickel.

The bust of Thomas Jefferson, whose efforts to establish a decimal system of coinage for the United States are still enjoyed today, was placed on the five-cent piece beginning in 1938. Jefferson's home, Monticello, is depicted on the reverse.

One interesting issue of 1939 shows doubling on both "Monticello" and "Five Cents." Another, struck in 1942, shows the "D" mintmark over a horizontal "D."

The 1939-D, with a mintage of 3.514 million, is generally considered the key date.

Wartime composition (1942-1945)

Composition: 56-percent copper, 35-percent silver (.0563 ounces), 9-percent manganese.

Need for the coinage metal nickel to aid in the war effort led to issuance in 1942 of a five-cent piece containing 35-percent silver.

In order to be able to readily identify the new five-cent pieces from those containing 25-percent nickel, the mintmark was placed prominantly above the dome of Monticello. For the first time a "P" was used to distinguish those coins struck at Philadelphia.

A significant overdate, the 1943/2-P, is known in the wartime composition.

Prewar composition resumed (1946 to date)

In 1946 coinage began again of the five-cent piece at the prewar composition of 75-percent copper and 25-percent copper. The mintmark was again placed to the side of Monticello.

The postwar series features a number of overmintmark coins, including the 1949-D/S, 1954-S/D, and the 1955-D/S.

In 1965 the Mint, facing a coinage shortage, opted to leave mintmarks off U.S. coins fearing, unjustly, that coin collectors were adding to the disappearance of coins from circulation.

Mintmarks would again be placed on U.S. coins beginning in 1968. On the five-cent piece the mintmark returned in larger form to a new location on the obverse.

In 1966 designer Felix Schlag's initials were added below the bust of Jefferson.

Specialists in the series often collect Jefferson nickels for the number and fullness of the porch steps on Monticello, which are generally weakly defined.

Modifications, noticeable in strengthening design details of Monticello, also led to the creation of collectible varieties in 1967, 1971 and 1977.

Striking Impressions

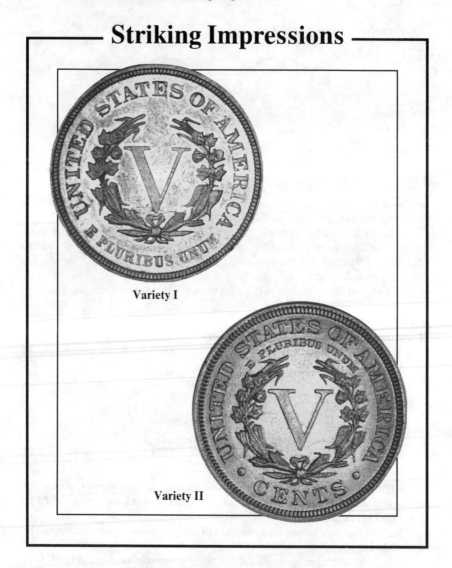

Variety I

Variety II

Racketeer nickel

When the Liberty Head nickel was introduced in 1883, the first issues bore only the Roman numeral "V" on the coin's reverse to indicate its value. The nickel's similarity in size and weight to a gold half eagle and the lack of the word "Cents" led to numerous pieces being gold plated and reeded so that the nickels could be passed as half eagles. These plated issues came to be known as racketeer nickels. Later that same year the problem was corrected by the addition of the word "Cents" below the wreath on the coin's reverse.

Striking Impressions

1913
Liberty Head nickel

Steeped in mystery when its existence was first revealed, the 1913 Liberty Head nickel is today one of the most famous of U.S. coins. Only five genuine specimens are known to exist, although numerous alterations have been produced by changing a digit of the date of a 1903, 1910, 1912 or other Liberty Head nickels. Besides its surreptitious production by a Mint employee — who would later promote the coin's existence and then try to sell his products at the 1920 American Numismatic Association convention — the 1913 Liberty Head nickel received further notoriety when, prior to World War II, Texas dealer B. Max Mehl offered to purchase for $50 any specimen discovered. Mehl's gimmick helped promote the sale of his coin catalog, but did not produce any additional examples. One specimen, now residing in the collection of the American Numismatic Association, as a result of a donation by Aubrey and Adeline Bebee, was famous as the coin Wisconsin dealer J.V. McDermott regularly carried in his pocket and displayed at bars and gave out on loan to coin clubs.

Striking Impressions

1911
Lincoln head nickel?

In 1911 James Earle Fraser produced an interesting coin design featuring the bust of Abraham Lincoln facing left. The idea for the design apparently originated with Philadelphia Mint Director George Roberts. In a June 13, 1911, letter from Fraser to the mint director Fraser wrote, "I think your idea of the Lincoln Head is a splendid one and I shall be glad to make some sketches as soon as possible and let you see them." Later that year Fraser submitted electrotypes for both an Indian Head nickel and his design of the Lincoln head. John W. Dunn suggested in an August 1976 article in *Coins* magazine, "Design for a Dream Coin," that Fraser's Lincoln head design may actually have been intended for a proposed aluminum three-cent piece. Either way, this interesting depiction of Lincoln was never employed on a U.S. coin and all that apparently remains is an 18.5 millimeter lead specimen, washed with copper and then silvered. At the time of Dunn's article this rare example of coinage history was on display at the National Cowboy Hall of Fame and Western Heritage Center in Oklahoma City, Okla.

Striking Impressions

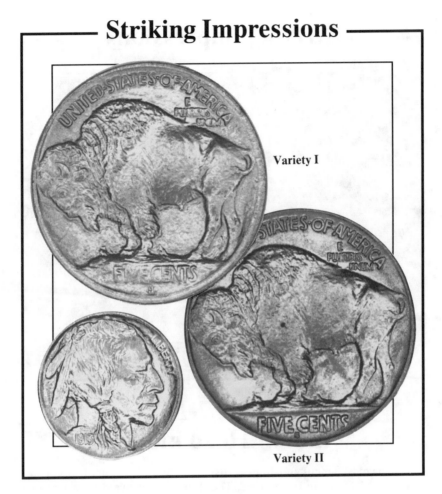

Variety I

Variety II

1913
Indian Head nickel

One of America's most popular coin designs — James Earle Fraser's Indian Head nickel — made its debut in 1913. This first year of issue witnessed the creation of two distinctly collectible varieties struck at the Philadelphia, Denver and San Francisco Mints. The 1913 Variety I coin shows the bison standing on raised ground. Once the coins entered circulation it was discovered that the demonination "Five Cents," which appeared on the face of the mound, would quickly wear down. The Variety II pieces were produced to correct that problem by displaying the bison on a straight line and placing the words "Five Cents" in recess. In most grades the Variety II coins carry a higher premium than the Variety I coins.

Striking Impressions

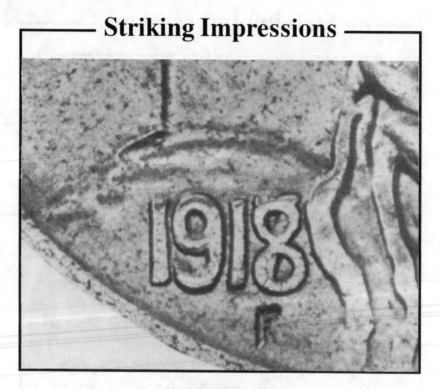

1918/7-D
Indian Head nickel

One of the most famous and dramatic overdates on 20th century U.S. coinage is the 1918/7-D Indian Head nickel. The clearly visible overdate was created when a 1917-dated die was inadvertently struck with a hub for the 1918 coinage. Only a single die is known to have been used. Even in the lowest grades, this rarity brings a high premium. Spurious examples created from normal 1917 or 1918 Denver nickels do exist. Authentication is recommended.

── Striking Impressions ──

Normal 1937-D reverse	**Three-legged reverse**

Three-legged
1937-D Indian Head nickel

A popular addition to any collection of Indian Head nickels is the 1937-D three-legged variety. This famous variety, which carries high premiums even in low grades, was caused by excessive grinding on the die to remove clash marks. The result the removal of the lower portion of the bison's front foreleg. The dies used to strike this variety were well-worn, making for a ragged appearance on the Indian's chin and the bison's hind leg and back. Normal 1937-D nickels that have been altered to pass for the three-legged variety exist and collectors should be wary. One helpful tip to distinguish the Mint-created 1937-D three-legged nickel from an altered four-legged 1937-D is the positioning of the "P" and "U" in "E Pluribus Unum" in relation to the bison's back. Note the additional distance between these two letters and the bison's back on the 1937-D three-legged nickel as compared to the normal four-legged 1937-D.

Striking Impressions

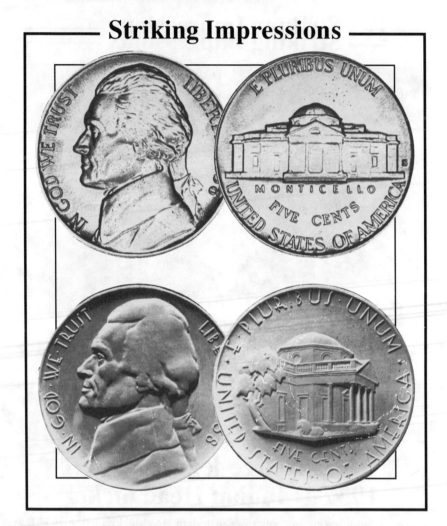

Jefferson nickel model

It is often interesting to look back at what might have been. For full-step Jefferson nickel collectors, the world would have been drastically changed if Felix Schlag's original model of Jefferson's Monticello had been accepted. In 1938 Schlag won a competition open to American sculptors to provide a new design for the U.S. five-cent piece, depicting Thomas Jefferson on one side and Monticello on the other. After running head-on into objections raised by the Commission of Fine Arts, Schlag was compelled to make revisions to both the obverse and reverse, eliminating the modernistic view of Jefferson's former home, reworking Jefferson's portrait, and changing the style of lettering.

Striking Impressions

Wartime nickels
1942-1945

The need for nickel as a strategic metal during World War II resulted in the introduction in 1942 of a five-cent piece comprised of 35-percent silver, 56-percent copper and 9-percent manganese. To readily distinguish the new wartime silver coin from its copper-nickel counterpart, a large mintmark was placed over the dome of Monticello on the coin's reverse. It was the first time a "P" was used to identify the coins of Philadelphia. Issued between 1942 and 1945, even heavily circulated war nickels command a slight premium because of the coin's 35-percent silver content.

Striking Impressions

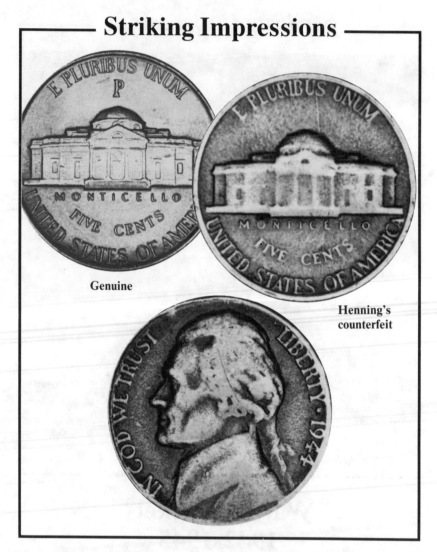

Genuine

Henning's
counterfeit

Henning's counterfeit nickel

One of the most famous counterfeits of the 20th century was that produced by Francis Leroy Henning during the early 1950s. Noted for being over-sized, overweight, of poor quality and color, and sporting a defect in the "R" of "Pluribus," Henning's 1944-dated nickels bore an even more glaring error. Henning failed to observe that genuine wartime silver nickels (1942-1945) displayed a mintmark above the dome of Monticello. Hennings, who turned to producing other non-silver dates as well before being arrested in 1955, was eventually sentenced to six years in jail and fined $5,000.

Striking Impressions

1943/2
Jefferson nickel

Discovered by Del Romines, the 1943/2 Jefferson nickel continues to cause some confusion. At the top is a photograph of a 1943 nickel with a die line sometimes mistaken for an example of this overdate. The lower photograph is that of the genuine 1943/2. Note the remainder of the numeral "2" following along the line of the bottom curl of the "3." Variety expert Alan Herbert observes that the left base of the "2" protrudes below the "3" and can be seen even on low-grade specimens of this overdate.

Dimes

Draped Bust (1797-1807)

Small-eagle reverse (1796-1797)

Designer: Robert Scot. **Size:** 19 millimeters. **Weight:** 2.7 grams. **Composition:** 89.24-percent silver (.0775 ounces), 10.76-percent copper.
Notes: 1797 strikes have either 13 or 16 stars on the obverse.

Coinage of dimes did not begin until 1796 by which time versions of Robert Scot's Draped Bust, modeled after a drawing by Gilbert Stuart, had already appeared on the silver dollar and were being adopted in that year for the cent, half dime and quarter dollar. The dime's reverse depicted a small eagle perched on a cloud enclosed by a wreath.

Mintages were low for both years of the small-eagle reverse, with 22,135 believed to have been struck bearing the 1796 date and an additional mintage of 25,261 in 1797.[1] Both dates are scarce, high-premium coins.

Heraldic-eagle reverse (1798-1807)

Notes: Varieties of the regular 1798 strikes are distinguished by the size of the "8" in the date. The 1805 strikes have either four or five berries on the olive branch held by the eagle.

Robert Scot's heraldic-eagle reverse was teamed with the Draped Bust obverse on the dime beginning in 1798.

Conservation of coinage dies at the first Mint often led to the creation of over-dates as a die prepared in a prior year was repunched and put into service. The 1798 strikes, for example, can be found with 98/97 and with 16 or 13 star obverses.

The 1804 is known with 13 stars or 14 stars on the reverse. The latter was created when a reverse for the 1804 quarter eagle was used on the dime coinage.

Most dates of this type were weakly struck. No dimes were coined in 1799 or 1806.

Capped Bust (1809-1837)

Large size (1809-1828)

Designer: John Reich. **Size:** 18.8 millimeters. **Weight:** 2.7 grams. **Composition:** 89.24-percent silver (.0775 ounces), 10.76-percent copper.
Notes: Varieties of the 1814, 1821, and 1828 strikes are distinguished by the size of the numerals in the dates. Varieties of 1820 are distinguished by the size of the "0" in the date. Overdates of 1823 have either large "E's" or small "E's" in "United States of America" on the reverse.

John Reich's Capped Bust design, which in 1807 had been placed on the half dollar, was introduced on the dime when coinage of that denomination resumed in 1809.

One of a number of interesting varieties occurred when the same reverse die with "StatesofAmerica" run together as one word was used in 1814 and again in 1820.

Coinage of the dime was sporadic. No dimes were struck in 1810, 1812-1813, 1815-1819, or in 1826.

The 1822, with a mintage of 100,000, is a key and scarce in all grades.

Reduced size (1828-1837)

Size: 18.5 millimeters.
Notes: Three varieties of 1829 strikes and two varieties of 1830 strikes are distinguished by the size of "10 C." on the reverse. An 1833 "high 3" variety has the last "3" in the date is higher than the first "3." Two varieties of the 1834 strikes are distinguished by the size of the "4" in the date.

The introduction of new equipment at the Mint and, in particular, the use of a closed coinage collar slightly reduced the diameter of the dime and made for more uniform coinage. The dime now also displayed a raised, beaded border.

Coinage of the dime, which prior to 1828 had been sporadic, became regular, with no breaks in the date run between 1828 and 1837.

Seated Liberty (1837-1891)

No stars (1837-1838)

Designer: Christian Gobrecht. **Size:** 17.9 millimeters. **Weight:** 2.67 grams. **Composition:** 90-percent silver (.0773 ounces), 10-percent copper.
Notes: Two 1837 varieties are distinguished by the size of the numerals in the date.

Christian Gobrecht's Seated Liberty design was placed on the dime in 1837 without the stars bordering the design that would characterize the issues from 1838-1860.

The rarest date of this type is the 1838-0, the first branch-mint coinage of dimes. With 406,034 struck, the 1838-0 is especially rare in uncirculated grades.

No dimes of this type were struck at Philadelphia in 1838, which had by then turned to coinage of the modified design with stars bordering Liberty.

Stars around rim (1838-1853)

Notes: Two 1838 varieties are distinguished by the size of the stars on the obverse. An 1838 "partial drapery" variety has drapery on Liberty's left elbow. An 1839-O with reverse of 1838-O variety was struck from rusted dies. This variety has a bumpy surface on the reverse.

Thirteen stars were added to the obverse design of Seated Liberty dimes beginning in 1838 on dimes struck at the Philadelphia Mint. Coinage of this type would not begin until the following year at the New Orleans facility.

The 1844, known to collectors as the "Orphan Annie" dime, is scarce; as is the 1846, which is lowest mintage date of this type with only 31,300 struck.

The Philadelphia Mint also struck 95,000 1853 "no arrow" coins at the old standard of 2.67 grams before the reduction of weight of the dime in that year to 2.49 grams.

Arrows at date (1853-1855)

Weight: 2.49 grams. Composition: 90-percent silver (.0721 ounces), 10-percent copper.

In 1853 the weight of the dime, along with other minor silver coins, was reduced in an attempt to keep silver in circulation. Large supplies of gold from the California gold fields had helped to drive the price of silver up to a point where silver coins were worth more as bullion than face value. Arrows were added at the date to dimes struck from 1853-1855 to denote the weight change.

First-year mintage of the "with arrows" dime was high at 12.078 million in Philadelphia. By contrast, only 1.1 million were struck in New Orleans.

Mintage at the Philadelphia Mint would drop to 4.47 million the following year, with the New Orleans coinage standing at 1.77 million. The final year of the "with arrows" dime included 2.075 million coins struck at the Philadelphia Mint.

All are relatively plentiful in lower grades.

Arrows at date removed (1856-1860)

Notes: Two 1856 varieties are distinguished by the size of the numerals in the date.

In 1856 the arrows were removed from the date area, even though the weight remained at the new, lower level. In that same year the San Francisco Mint struck its first dime, with a low mintage of 60,000. This date and the like mintage 1859-S are scarce in all grades.

Although in 1860 Philadelphia and New Orleans began striking the new Seated Liberty type (with the legend "United States of America" replacing the stars on the obverse) San Francisco continued to mint the old type, producing its largest mintage of dimes up to that point at 140,000.

Obverse legend (1860-1873)

Notes: 1873 "closed-3" and "open-3" varieties are known and are distinguished by the amount of space between the upper left and lower left serifs of the "3" in the date.

In 1860 chief engraver James B. Longacre reworked the design of the dime on orders of Mint Director A. Loudon Snowden. The inscription "United States of America" was moved to the obverse and a new so-called cereal wreath was placed on the reverse.

A number of rarities exist of this type, including the Carson City issues of 1871-1872 and a unique 1873-CC dime without arrows. In the case of the latter, although Mint records indicate that some 12,400 were struck, only one is known to exist, having been traced to once having been in the possession of Mint Director Snowden.

All of the Philadelphia dates from 1863-1867 were low mintage and are scarce in all grades. By contrast, San Francisco mintages of the dime were high during the same period. For example, in 1867, while the Philadelphia Mint struck a mere 6,625 dimes, the San Francisco facility coined some 140,000.

Arrows at date (1873-1874)

Weight: 2.5 grams. Composition: 90-percent silver (.0724 ounces), 10- percent copper.

As part of the Coinage Act of 1873, later dubbed the "Crime of 1873" for its failure to include provision to coin a 412.5-grain silver dollar, attempts were made to adjust minor silver coinage to a metric standard. International monetary schemes, whereby standard weights in grams would be employed, were in vogue at the time.

The weight of the dime was raised to 2.50 grams to place it on a metric standard. Arrows were added to the date area of dimes struck in 1873 and 1874 to mark the increase in weight.

The Carson City dates of this type are the rarest, with a mintage of just 18,791 in 1873 and 10,817 struck in 1874.

Arrows at date removed (1875-1891)

Notes: On a 1876-CC doubled-obverse variety, doubling appears in the words "of America" in the legend.

In 1875 the arrows, placed by the date in 1873 to designate the change in weight of the dime to a metric standard, were dropped.

Mintages of dimes, even at the Carson City Mint, were heavy into 1878 when all minor coins took a beating with the passage of the Bland-Allison Act. This act - a minor victory for the forces of free silver (who wanted the reinstatement of the standard 412.5-grain dollar dropped by the Coinage Act of 1873) - forced the Mint to turn its attention to striking the new silver dollar.

Coinage of the dime, which had in prior years stood at 7.7 million, fell to 200,000 in 1878. The coinage dropped even more dramatically from 1879-1881, with scant mintages of 15,100, 37,355 and 24,975, respectively, from the Philadelphia Mint and no dimes struck at the branch mints. These dates are scarce in all grades.

The 1885-S, with a mintage of 43,690, is also scarce in all grades.

Barber (1892-1916)

Designer: Charles E. Barber. **Size:** 17.9 millimeters. **Weight:** 2.5 grams. **Composition:** 90-percent silver (.0724 ounces), 10-percent copper.

Mint chief engraver Charles Barber's design of a capped Liberty head was placed on the dime in 1892. It was also placed on the quarter and half dollar that same year.

First-year mintages of Barber dimes were high, as the Philadelphia Mint churned out 12.121 million and the New Orleans and San Francisco facilities contributed 3.841 million and 990,710, respectively.

Although the 1895-0, with a mintage of 440,000, is the series' regular-issue key and scarce in all grades, the most famous Barber dime is the 1894-S of which only 24 were struck in proof. Theories vary as to why only 24 dimes were struck. One that seems to make sense is that New Orleans Mint superintendent Hallie Daggett had the coins struck as special gifts for banking friends.[2] Only about one dozen 1894-S dimes are known to exist today.

Mercury (1916-1945)

Designer: Adolph A. Weinman. **Size:** 17.9 millimeters. **Weight:** 2.5 grams. **Composition:** 90-percent silver (.0724 ounces), 10-percent copper.
Notes: A 1945-S "micro" variety has a smaller mintmark than the normal variety.

In 1916, as part of the wave of coinage redesign inspired by President Theodore Roosevelt, the winged Liberty or Mercury design, as it is commonly known today, was introduced. This design remains one of the most popular of all U.S. coins.

This series includes the notable 20th-century overdates, the 1942/1 and 1942/1-D.

The most famous date, however, is the 1916-D, which carries high premiums in, and is sought, even in low grades. It had a series' low mintage of 264,000. Also in demand, even in low grades, are the 1921 and 1921-D.

Roosevelt (1946 to date)

Silver composition (1946-1964)

Designer: John R. Sinnock. **Size:** 17.9 millimeters. **Weight:** 2.5 grams. **Composition:** 90-percent silver (.0724 ounces), 10-percent copper.

Released in honor of President Franklin D. Roosevelt, the Roosevelt dime continued the trend toward placing portraits of presidents and statesmen on U.S. coins. The cent, nickel, and quarter had already abandoned representations of Liberty in favor of depictions of Abraham Lincoln, Thomas Jefferson and George Washington, respectively.

The half dollar would follow, in 1948, with Benjamin Franklin. When the dollar coin was reintroduced in 1971 it featured Dwight D. Eisenhower.

The 1949-S Roosevelt dime, with a mintage of 13.510 million, is generally considered the series' key.

Clad composition (1965 to date)

Weight: 2.27 grams. **Composition:** clad layers of 75-percent copper and 25-percent nickel, bonded to a pure-copper core.
Notes: A 1979-S Type II proof has a clearer mintmark than the Type I.

Faced with rising silver prices and a coinage shortage, the Mint dropped silver from the dime in 1965, replacing it with a base-metal clad composition, featuring an inner core of 100-percent copper. In 1982 a portion of the mintage included dimes missing the "P" mintmark. These command a strong premium. A portion of the mintage of annual government proof sets in 1968, 1970, 1975 and 1983 is known to have contained premium dimes lacking the proper "S" mintmark.

—— Striking Impressions ——

1859
Transitional
dime and half dime

An interesting muling of the regular obverse of 1859 and the regular reverse of 1860 resulted in the creation of a small number of proof half dimes and dimes that failed to display the required legend "United States of America."

Striking Impressions

'Orphan Annie' dime

Collectors have often given colorful nicknames to coins such as the Silly Head, Booby Head and Petite Head descriptions employed for varieties of the 1839 large cent. One of the most famous nicknames is that given to the 1844 dime. Legend has it that during the 1930s the late Frank C. Ross, who wrote a column on coins for *Hobbies* magazine, promoted the 1844 Seated Liberty dime as being a truly scarce coin while, according to Walter Breen, hoarding examples of the low-mintage date. Ross deemed the coin the "Orphan Annie" because it "had no buyers and was just an orphan in the coin world."

Striking Impressions

Type I   Type II

1861 dime
Type I and Type II shields

Modification of the coinage dies in 1860 led to the creation of the Type I or "five lines" shield and the Type II "six lines" shield on the 1861 Philadelphia Seated Liberty dime. The Type I specimens show only five vertical lines in the area directly above "ERTY" in "Liberty." The Type II shield with six lines came into use exclusively in 1862. The 1861 Type I variety is considered scarcer than the Type II.

── Striking Impressions ──

Diagnostic:
1894-S dime

The 1894-S dime is undeniably one of the most famous rarities in the U.S. coinage series. Only 12 of the original mintage of 24 are believed to exist. As with most rarities, altered examples exist. Many were produced by adding an "S" mintmark to an 1894 dime or by altering an 1894-0. The offering of an undocumented 1894-S should be considered suspect and all examples authenticated. The known genuine specimens display minute die chips at the base and top of the "E" in "Dime."

Striking Impressions

Mercury dime

Adolph A. Weinman's design for the obverse of the dime issued from 1916-1945 mistakenly led the coin to be known as the "Mercury" dime. His Liberty head with wings brought to mind common depictions of the Roman god Mercury. Mercury was often portrayed wearing a winged hat and winged sandals. Weinman, however, never meant for this association to occur. In a Nov. 14, 1916, dated letter from Frank G. Duffield, editor of *The Numismatist* (reprinted in the December issue of *The Numismatist*), Weinman explained the meaning of his design, writing that "the wings crowning her [Liberty's] cap are intended to symbolize liberty of thought." The fasces on the reverse, he said, were "to symbolize the strength which lies in unity, while the battle-ax stands for preparedness to defend the Union. The branch of olive is symbolical of our love of peace."

Striking Impressions

Diagnostic:
1942/1 Mercury dime

One helpful tip in determining the authenticity of a 1942/1 Mercury dime is the positioning of the "R" in the word "Liberty" in relation to the wing. Mercury dimes dated 1941 and before show the right leg of the "R" touching the wing. On Mercury dimes from 1942 through 1945, it does not touch. Coins altered from a 1942 to a 1942/1 will show a space at this point.

Striking Impressions

Diagnostic:
1942/1
Mercury dime

One of the most dramatic overdates of the 20th century, the 1942/1 Mercury dime was not discovered until a year after its release, thus accounting for the number of worn specimens available today. Be particularly careful in purchasing specimens of this overdate, because numerous forgeries exist. Authentication is recommended. Some helpful characteristics displayed by genuine examples include the doubling of the numeral "4," a tiny spur connected to the number "9," shooting off toward the top of the "4," and die scratches below the "4." Also note that the numeral "1" appears to the left of the "2" and is slightly lower on genuine examples.

20-cent

(1875-1878)

Designer: William Barber. **Size:** 22 millimeters. **Weight:** 5 grams. **Composition:** 90-percent silver (.1447 ounces), 10-percent copper.

One of the shortest-lived series of U.S. coins, the 20-cent piece was ostensibly the brain-child of Nevada Senator John Percival Jones, friend of silver-mining interests. Jones had argued in favor of the 20-cent denomination to alleviate problems with making change in the West, where a lack of minor coins often caused the purchaser of lower-priced items to be shortchanged in transactions involving a quarter.

Its placement at a weight of five grams, it was believed, would make the 20-cent piece convenient as an international coin as well, fitting in with the other silver coins, which had been adjusted upward in weight to a metric standard in 1873. The size and resemblance of the 20-cent piece to the Seated Liberty quarter, however, led to confusion and brought about its elimination as a coinage denomination in 1878.

The first year of mintage was the largest, with 1.155 million struck at the San Francisco Mint, an additional 133,290 minted in Carson City, and a low 39,700 struck at the parent mint in Philadelphia.

After that, mintage of the 20-cent piece dropped sharply to 15,900 in 1876 in Philadelphia and 10,000 at Carson City. The latter is a great rarity, as most were melted at the Mint. Less than two dozen specimens are believed to have escaped the melting pot. Only proofs were struck in 1877 (350) and 1878 (600).

Unlike the dimes, quarters, half dollars and silver dollar of the period, the edge of the 20-cent piece was plain (not reeded) and the word "Liberty" was raised on the surface rather than recessed.

Striking Impressions

1876-CC 20-cent piece

The 1876-CC 20-cent piece is by far the greatest rarity in this short-lived coinage series. The termination of the half dime by the Coinage Act of 1873 and a general shortage of minor coinage in the West led Sen. John Percival Jones, R-Nev., to introduce a bill in February 1874 calling for a 20-cent coin. The new denomination was expected to alleviate problems with daily transactions. As merchants often priced items at 10 cents, customers paying with a quarter dollar were generally short-changed, being forced to take a dime in change and forfeit five cents. Because of its similarity in size to the quarter dollar, the 20-cent piece was immediately rejected by the public and was only coined for circulation in 1875-1876. In 1877, at the order of Mint Director Henry R. Linderman, the remaining supply of Carson City 20-cent pieces were melted. The 1876-CC was a casualty of the melt. Of the original mintage of 10,000 coins, as few as 18 are thought to exist. All genuine specimens show distinct doubling on the word "Liberty" appearing on Liberty's shield.

Quarters

Draped Bust (1796-1807)

Small-eagle reverse (1796)

Designer: Robert Scot. **Size:** 27.5 millimeters. **Weight:** 6.74 grams. **Composition:** 89.24-percent silver (.1935 ounces), 10.76-percent copper.

Even though it was authorized by the Coinage Act of 1792, coinage of the quarter dollar did not begin until four years later. Featured on this low mintage (6,146) and rare one-year type was Robert Scot's Draped Bust design with small-eagle reverse, already in use on the large cent, half dime, half dollar and silver dollar.

Heraldic-eagle reverse (1804-1807)

After a hiatus of eight years, coinage of the quarter dollar began again in 1804, this time with the heraldic-eagle reverse, and for the first time expressing the denomination, shown as "25 C" on the reverse.

First-year coinage of the Draped Bust quarter with heraldic eagle was a miniscule 6,738. Thereafter, mintages increased to 121,394, 206,124 and 220,643, respectively, for 1805-1807 coinage. All of which, though not as high priced as the 1804, carry significant premiums in all states of preservation.

Capped Bust (1815-1838)

Large size (1815-1828)

Designer: John Reich. **Size:** 27 millimeters. **Weight:** 6.74 grams. **Composition:** 89.24-percent silver (.1935 ounces), 10.76-percent copper.
Notes: Varieties of the 1819 strikes are distinguished by the size of the "9" in the date. Varieties of the 1820 strikes are distinguished by the size of the "0" in the date.

Coinage of the quarter dollar was often sporadic at the first Mint. No quarters were struck from 1808-1814. When the quarter was reintroduced in 1815 it carried the Capped Bust design credited to John Reich.

Due to the necessity of preserving die steel many overdates exist in this type.

One of the more interesting varieties is the "25 over 50 C," which appears on some 1822 and 1828-dated quarters. Apparently the engraver blundered by placing the wrong denomination on the die then corrected his mistake. After being used in 1822, the same die was again employed in 1828, despite the obvious mistake.

Two great rarities of the series are the 1823/2 and the 1827/3. Of the former, less than two dozen are believed to exist out of an original mintage of more than 17,000. Of the 1827/3, only 10 are traced in proof, with an additional dozen or so restrikes known, having been produced more than 30 years later from scrapped mint dies.

Small size (1831-1838)

Designer: William Kneass. **Size:** 24.3 millimeters.
Notes: Varieties of the 1831 strikes are distinguished by the size of the lettering on the reverse.

Use of a closed coinage collar, introduced at the Mint in late 1820s, created a smaller diameter quarter - down from 27 millimeters to 24.3 millimeters. Another readily noticeable change to the design was the introduction of a raised border and the removal of the motto "E Pluribus Unum" from above the eagle.

Seated Liberty (1838-1891)

No motto (1838-1853)

Designer: Christian Gobrecht. **Size:** 24.3 millimeters. **Weight:** 6.68 grams. **Composition:** 90-percent silver (.1934 ounces), 10-percent copper.
Notes: 1852 obverse dies were used to strike the 1853 no-arrows variety, with the "2" being recut to form a "3."

The adoption of Christian Gobrecht's Seated Liberty design for the quarter dollar was part of an overall trend toward uniformity of design of all U.S. silver coins. In 1840 Robert Ball Hughes modified the design including an extra fold of drapery from Liberty's left elbow.

The 1840-0 is known in both "no drapery" and "drapery" varieties. In 1842 the date size was enlarged and two rarities resulted - the 1842 small date in proof, of which only six specimens are known, and the 1842-0 circulation issue, which is generally found in low grades. Also rare are the 1849-0, 1852-0 and 1853 without arrows and rays.

Arrows at date, reverse rays (1853)

Weight: 6.68 grams. **Composition:** 90-percent silver (.18 ounces), 10-percent copper.

In 1853 the quarter dollar joined the half dime, dime, and half dollar in sporting arrows next to the date to mark the reduction in weight associated with the passage of the Act of 1853. The quarter dollar and half dollar also showed a glory of rays around the eagle on the reverse.

The silver dollar was the only silver coin unaffected by the change, as its weight remained at the 412.5-grain standard.

This, however, led to lower mintages of the silver dollar and its constant hoarding and melting.

A popular one-year type coin, the "arrows and rays" quarter was struck at Philadelphia in a mintage of more than 15 million and at New Orleans with a mintage of more than 1.3 million.

An 1853/1854 overdate is known.

Reverse rays removed (1854-1855)

Notes: An 1854-O "huge O" variety has an oversized mintmark.

In 1854 the rays were removed from the reverse design of quarter, but the arrows remained, still signaling the reduction in weight first implemented in 1853. The use of this design type continued through 1855 with the branch-mint issues of New Orleans (176,000) and San Francisco (396,400) being scarce.

1855 also marked the first year of mintage of the quarter dollar at San Francisco.

Arrows at date removed (1856-1865)

In 1856 the arrows were omitted from the date area of the quarter, but the weight remained at the new, lower level mandated by the Act of 1853. Branch-mint issues of this type generally had the lowest mintages and bring the strongest premiums in all grades. The 1860-S and 1864-S are scarce.

After banks suspended specie payments late in 1860 (not to be restored until 1878) precious metals were hoarded. Production of all silver coins at the Philadelphia Mint suffered.

From a high of 7.368 million in 1858, coinage of quarters at the parent mint plummeted to 59,300 by 1865, making later Philadelphia business strikes scarce.[1]

Motto above eagle (1866-1873)

Notes: 1873 "closed-3" and "open-3" varieties are known and are distinguished by the amount of space between the upper left and lower left serifs in the "3."

The addition of a religious motto to the nation's coinage was first suggested by Rev. M. R. Watkinson of Pennsylvania and, after experimentation with several variations, the motto "In God We Trust" was adopted. It first appeared on the two-cent piece in 1864 and in 1866 on the half dollar, silver dollar and gold denominations above the quarter eagle.

Included in this type are several low-mintage issues of Carson City. The Nevada facility, located only a short distance from silver-rich Comstock Lode, began striking quarters in 1870 with a scant mintage of 8,340, a high-premium date in all grades. Also very scarce are the 1871-1873 "CC" dates. The 1873-CC, with a mintage of 4,000, is a classic rarity of which only three examples are known to exist.

High prices of silver following the Civil War also kept mintages generally well below 100,000 per year at the Philadelphia and San Francisco mints throughout the first five years of issuance of this type. The 1866, with a mintage of just 17,525, is a high-priced key, as are the 1871-S and 1872-S coins.

Arrows at date (1873-1874)

Weight: 6.25 grams.

The Coinage Act of 1873, the first major overhaul of mint laws since 1792, increased the weight of the quarter from 6.22 grams to 6.25 grams. The move was motivated by a prevalent talk of international coinage based on the metric system and had the support of several influential people, including John Jay Knox, framer of the Coinage Act of 1873.

Although mintage was more than 1.2 million at the Philadelphia Mint during 1873, the Carson City Mint struck only 12,462 quarters, making the 1873-CC "arrows" quarter rare.

Arrows at date removed (1875-1891)

In 1875 the arrows, which marked the increase in the weight of the quarter dollar in 1873, were removed from its design.

Mintages at the Philadelphia Mint were high, reaching 17.817 million in 1876 and continuing strong until 1879, when the Bland-Allison Act, passed the year prior, forced the Mint to turn its attention to the production of silver dollars. From a mintage of 2.26 million in 1878, coinage at the Philadelphia facility dropped to 14,700 in 1879 and hovered in that range or lower until 1891, the last year of the Seated Liberty design.

Besides the low-mintage Philadelphia strikes, branch-mint coinage of this type was often small. Scarce dates include the 1875-CC (140,000), 1878-S (140,000) and 1891-0 (68,000).

The 1891-0 was also the only Seated Liberty quarter from that mint to carry the motto "In God We Trust."

Barber (1892-1916)

Designer: Charles E. Barber. **Size:** 24.3 millimeters. **Weight:** 6.25 grams. **Composition:** 90-percent silver (.1809 ounces), 10-percent copper.

Charles Barber's capped Liberty replaced the Seated Liberty design in 1892. A heraldic eagle occupied the reverse.

The Barber quarter was struck at the Philadelphia, New Orleans and San Francisco mints. Key dates include 1896-S (188,039), 1901-S (72,664) and 1913-S (40,000).

Standing Liberty (1916-1930)

Type I (1916-1917)

Designer: Hermon A. MacNeil. **Size:** 24.3 millimeters. **Weight:** 6.25 grams. **Composition:** 90-percent silver (.1809 ounces), 10-percent copper.

Hermon A. MacNeil, a noted sculptor of American Indians, was a winner, along with Adolph A. Weinman, of a design competition that saw the introduction of new designs on the dime, quarter and half dollar.

MacNeil's design of a standing Liberty with shield raised in defense made its way on to the quarter in 1916.

Long-held belief has it that public outcry against the partial nudity of the design led to a modification in early 1917 to cover Liberty's breast. Letters written by MacNeil, however, suggest that in the end it was the artist who favored the design change. [2] Whatever the reason, this two-year type is very popular.

Striking problems were prevalent through much of this series and many dates are notorious for being found weakly struck, especially in the design detail of Liberty's head.

The 1916, with a mintage of 52,000, is rare in all grades.

Type II (1917-1924)

Beginning in 1917 the design of the quarter was changed to include a chain-mail covering over the exposed right breast of Liberty.

This design type includes the 1918/1917-S overdate, one of the most dramatic in a limited number of 20th-century overdates. The 1923-S is a key in all grades and rare with fully struck head detail. No quarters were minted in 1922.

Recessed date (1925-1930)

From the outset of coinage one of the major problems with the design of the quarter was the positioning of the date on a raised level. In 1925 the design was modified to place the date in recess and protect it from wear.

The 1926-S is a notable rarity with full head detail, as is the 1930-S. The 1927-S, with a mintage of 396,000, is a key date.

Washington (1932 to date)

Silver composition (1932-1964)

Designer: John Flanagan. **Size:** 24.3 millimeters. **Weight:** 6.25 grams. **Composition:** 90-percent silver (.1809 ounces), 10-percent copper.

The bicentennial of the birth of President George Washington was the motivation behind the introduction of the Washington quarter in 1932. Despite selection by judging commissions of a design by Laura Gardin Fraser, wife of Indian Head nickel designer James Earle Fraser, the influence of Secretary of the Treasury Andrew Mellon led to John Flanagan's modeling of Houdon bust of Washington being used on the quarter dollar. [3]

The 1932-D and -S strikes are keys. Other dates have proven elusive in gem-uncirculated condition.

Varieties include the 1934 light- and heavy-motto pieces, 1934 doubled die, 1943-S doubled-die obverse, and two curious overmintmark pieces - the 1950-D/S and 1950-S/D.

Clad composition (1965 to date)

Weight: 5.67 grams. **Composition:** clad layers of 75-percent copper and 25-percent nickel bonded to a pure-copper core.

In 1965 silver was removed from all circulating coins, with the exception of the half dollar. Replacing the former 90-percent silver, 10-percent copper composition was a new sandwich metal, comprised of outer layers of 75-percent copper and 25-percent nickel and an inner core of 100-percent copper.

The Coinage Act of 1965 also discontinued the use of mintmarks, which were not restored to coinage until 1968 by which time the mintmark position was moved from the reverse of the quarter to the obverse.

Bicentennial reverse (1975-1976)

Reverse designer: Jack L. Ahr.

The U.S. Bicentennial celebration resulted in the creation of new designs for the reverse of quarter, half dollar and Eisenhower dollar. An open design competition was held and Jack L. Ahr's depiction of a Colonial drummer boy was selected for the quarter dollar.

Struck in 1975 and 1976, Bicentennial quarters bear the distinctive dating "1776-1976."

Regular design resumed (1977 to date)

The eagle reverse returned to the quarter dollar in 1977, in a slightly lower relief, and continues in use today.

Striking Impressions

Curled base 2

Square base 2

1827/3 Capped Bust proof quarter

In 1827 Joseph J. Mickley walked into the Philadelphia Mint and obtained four 1827/3 proof quarters in exchange for a dollar. Those were the only specimens known for several decades. Today, 10 original examples are thought to exist. The specimen shown is one of the four obtained by Mickley. It appeared in Auctions by Bowers and Merena's March 24-25, 1988, sale of the Norweb collection where it sold for $61,600, including a 10-percent buyer's fee. Restrikes were produced during the late 1850s using a cracked 1819 reverse die and an 1827 obverse die. Twelve restrikes have been traced. The originals can be easily distinguished by the base of the "2" in the denomination on the reverse. It is curled on the originals and square on the restrikes.

── Striking Impressions ──

Type I

Type II

Type I and Type II
Standing Liberty quarters

When sculptor Hermon MacNeil's design for the quarter appeared on the coins of 1916, the first specimens showed a full-length figure of Liberty with an exposed right breast. This Type I modeling for Liberty appeared on the issues dated 1916 and the early strikings of 1917. In 1917 a Type II modeling of Liberty was substituted. On subsequent coins, Liberty wears a chain-mail garment that discretely covers the upper portion of her body.

Striking Impressions

Type I

Type II

Standing Liberty quarter

Though most public and collector attention focused on the changes to the dress of the obverse figure of Liberty when modifications were made to the Standing Liberty quarter design in early 1917, the reverse also went through some changes. Designer Hermon A. MacNeil had complained to Mint director F.J.H. von Engelken that on the first coins released (Type I) the eagle had been dropped too low, which made it look, when soiled, as if the tail was connected with the lettering below. MacNeil suggested that the Mint may have made the change to prevent the eagle's right wing from touching the "A" in "America," a feature he liked and which would return on the modified Type II design. He also complained that lowering the eagle gave the appearance of a low-flying or just-rising eagle, and that from his study of the bird, the talons are ony extended behind when the eagle is well underway at high altitude. As it appeared on the Type II coins, the eagle was raised and the lettering was respaced with three of the 13 design stars placed below the eagle.

— Striking Impressions —

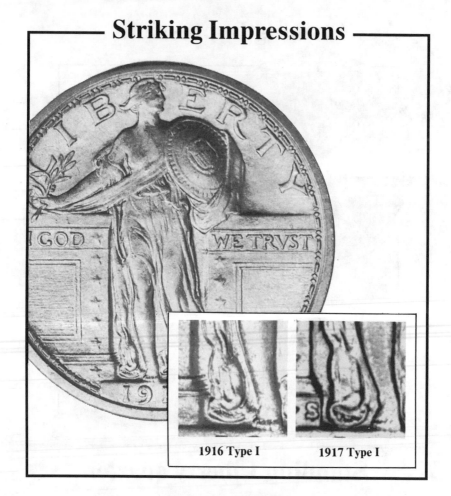

1916 Type I   1917 Type I

Diagnostic:
Standing Liberty quarter

The former American Numismatic Association Certification Service use to stress that one method of avoiding altered coins is to know the diagnostics of genuine coins. One such helpful tip was provided by the ANA in the October 1981 issue of *The Numismatist*. On the 1916 Type I quarter, the lower fold of Liberty's gown is slightly rounded and almost flat across the bottom. This same drapery fold is oval shaped on the 1917 Type I quarter. The 1916 Type I quarter carries significant premiums in all grades over its 1917 Type I counterpart. This diagnostic is helpful in detecting a 1916-dated quarter created by altering the digit "7" to a "6" on a 1917 Philadelphia Type I coin.

Striking Impressions

1921 Standing Liberty quarter

The 1921 Standing Liberty quarter carries significant premium even in lower grades. Any coin that carries a strong premium even its lowest states of preservation is subject to alteration. A popular tool for this purpose has been the lower-valued 1924 Standing Liberty quarter — changing the "4" to a "1" to create a coin that could unscrupulously be passed to collectors as an original 1921 quarter. Close examination should reveal such alteration, but another tip is to take note of the style of the first "1" in the date of the 1921 quarter and the 1924 coin. The "1" on the 1921 quarter is thicker than that found on the later-date and lower-priced 1924 quarter and should help in the detection of altered coins.

Striking Impressions

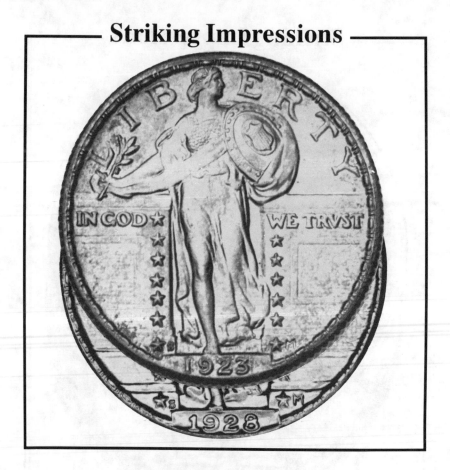

Diagnostic:
1923-S Standing Liberty quarter

The 1923-S is one of the key dates in the Standing Liberty quarter series and as such commands a hefty premium even in lower grades. The chance to make something out of nothing often leads to alteration of less valuable dates in the hope of deceiving unsuspecting collectors. One of the more common form of deceptions associated with the 1923-S quarter is the alteration of the "8" on a 1928-S to a "3." This alteration is easily identified because in 1925 the design of the Standing Liberty quarter was changed to show the date area in recess in order to protect the date from wear. Coins altered from a 1928-S quarter will show the date in recess, whereas, an original 1923-S displays a raised date. On a genuine 1923-S the top of the "3" in the date is flat. The top of the "3" would appear rounded if altered from a 1928-S.

Striking Impressions

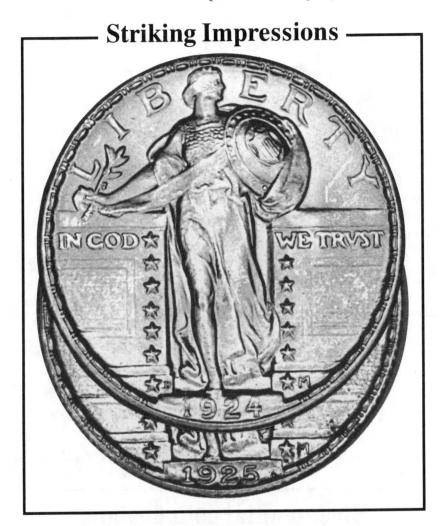

Standing Liberty quarter
Recessed date

First released in 1916, it took nine years before the Mint changed the positioning of the date on the Standing Liberty quarter. It was an attempt to stop the problem of circulation wear, which had led to large numbers of dateless Standing Liberty quarters. In 1925 the design was modified to remove the date from the raised panel on which it formerly rested, placing it in recess to protect it from circulation wear. The series continued with the recessed date through 1930.

——— Striking Impressions ———

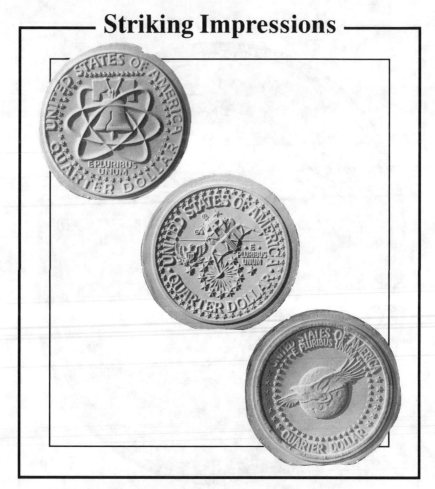

Bicentennial coin designs

It was truly a design competition open to the people. Approximately 1,000 artists, including school students, entered the open competition for the nation's Bicentennial coinage designs. The competition for the special commemorative reverses of the quarter, half and dollar coins brought out a wide variety of artistic styles and representations. A committee of the National Sculpture Society was then given the task of narrowing the field to 12 semi-finalists, which was further broken down to six finalists. The plaster models highlighted above are works of the three finalists, whose models narrowly missed being accepted for the dual-dated (1776-1976) Bicentennial coins. From the top, the artists were Prof. Ogden Dalrymple of Sioux Falls, S.D.; Dean McMullen of Portland, Ore.; and Brydon Stewart of Yakima, Wash.

Half dollars

Flowing Hair (1794-1795)

Designer: Robert Scot. **Size:** 32.5 millimeters. **Weight:** 13.48 grams. **Composition:** 89.24-percent silver (.3869 ounces), 10.76-percent copper.

Robert Scot's Flowing Hair design, with small-eagle reverse, graced the nation's first half dollar as it did the half dime and dollar in that same year. Minus the liberty cap and pole, the obverse design was much the same as that, which also appeared on the half cent and large cent.

As the dies were largely engraved by hand, many varieties exist. Many pieces also exhibit adjustment marks, file markings caused at the Mint as overweight planchets were brought to the proper weight.

The 1794 is the scarcest date of this type with 23,464 minted.

Draped Bust (1796-1807)

Small-eagle reverse (1796-1797)

Designer: Robert Scot. **Size:** 32.5 millimeters. **Weight:** 13.48 grams. **Composition:** 89.24-percent silver (.3869 ounces), 10.76-percent copper.
Notes: The 1796 strikes have either 15 or 16 stars on the obverse.

With a combined mintage of under 4,000 for the 1796 and 1797 dates, the Draped Bust half dollar with small-eagle reverse is a true rarity and accordingly priced even in the lowest grades. The design is credited to Mint engraver Robert Scot after a drawing by celebrated painter Gilbert Stuart. Stuart is probably best known to Americans for his famed painting of first president George Washington.

The Draped Bust design, adopted in 1796 for use on all silver and copper coins, with the exception of the half cent, was employed through 1807 before giving way to designs by John Reich.

Heraldic-eagle reverse (1801-1807)

Notes: Two varieties of the 1803 strikes are distinguished by the size of the "3" in the date. The several varieties of the 1806 strikes are distinguished by the style of "6" in the date, size of the stars on the obverse, and whether the stem of the olive branch held by the reverse eagle extends through the claw.

When half-dollar coinage resumed in 1801, Scot's heraldic eagle had replaced his small-eagle design on the coin's reverse.

Varieties are plentiful, including an 1805/4 overdate made especially interesting as no half dollars were minted bearing an 1804 date.

Because of the high relief of the Draped Bust obverse, many of the dates of this type exhibit strike weakness on the reverse.

Capped Bust (1807-1839)

Lettered edge (1807-1836)

Designer: John Reich. **Size:** 32.5 millimeters. **Weight:** 13.48 grams. **Composition:** 89.24-percent silver (.3869 ounces), 10.76-percent copper.

Notes: Two varieties of the 1807 strikes are distinguished by the size of the stars on the obverse. Two varieties of the 1811 are distinguished by the size of the "8" in the date. A third has a period between the "8" and second "1" in the date. One variety of the 1817 has a period between the "1" and "7" in the date. Two varieties of the 1819/18 overdate are distinguished by the size of the "9" in the date. Two varieties of the 1820 are distinguished by the size of the date. On 1823 varieties, the "broken 3" appears to be almost separated in the middle of the "3" in the date; the "patched 3" has the error repaired; the "ugly 3" has portions of its detail missing. The 1827 "curled-2" and "square-2" varieties are distinguished by the numeral's base — either curled or square. Among 1828 varieties, "knobbed 2" and "no knob" refers to whether the upper left serif of the digit is rounded. 1830 varieties are distinguished by the size of the "0" in the date. The four 1834 varieties are distinguished by the sizes of the stars, date and letters in the inscriptions. 1836 "50/00" variety was struck from a reverse die that had "50" recut over "00" in the denomination.

John Reich's design appeared, replacing that of Robert Scot, on the half dollar beginning in 1807. Blundered dies and varieties are the rule in this type, not the exception. Much of the operations at the first Mint were done by hand and open to human error.

One of the more interesting is the 1807 with "50," representing the denomination, punched over "20."

Some varieties involve slight variations, others are dramatic. In 1813, for example, an engraver placed the denomination "50 C" over "Uni," apparently to correct improper positioning of the beginning of "United States." On an 1814 strike an "E" had to be punched over the letter "A" in "States" to correct the spelling.

So numerous are the varieties that a specialized club, the Bust Half Nut Club, exists and requires the assembly of a set containing a high number of the varieties in order to gain membership.

Scarce dates include the 1815/2 and 1817/4 strikes.

Reeded edge, "50 Cents" on reverse (1836-1837)

Designer: Christian Gobrecht. **Size:** 30 millimeters. **Weight:** 13.36 grams. **Composition:** 90-percent silver (.3867 ounces), 10-percent copper.

Adoption of a closed coinage collar, which came into use at the Mint beginning in late 1820s, led to use of a reeded edge on the half dollar in place of the former lettered edge. Unlike the lettered edge, which had to be applied before striking by a separate machine using segmented collars, reeding would be applied at time of striking as the metal flowed into the collar.

The denomination now read "50 Cents," whereas on prior Bust halves it had been represented as "50 C."

Mintage in 1836 of the reeded-edge half dollar was low, at slightly more than 1,000. Type collectors looking to save money may want to opt for the less expensive and more plentiful 1837 strike of which 3.7 million were minted.

"Half Dol." on reverse (1838-1839)

In 1838 the denomination was again changed, this time from "50 Cents" to "Half Dol."

In that year the first branch-mint coinage of half dollars began with the striking of 20 proofs at the newly established mint in New Orleans. About 10 examples of this great rarity are known to exist today.

Seated Liberty (1839-1891)

No motto above eagle (1839-1853)

Designer: Christian Gobrecht. **Size:** 30.6 millimeters. **Weight:** 13.36 grams. **Composition:** 90-percent silver (.3867 ounces), 10-percent copper.
Notes: One variety of the 1840 strikes has smaller lettering; another used the old reverse of 1838. Varieties of 1842 and 1846 are distinguished by the size of the numerals in the date.

Introduced in 1836 on the dollar, the Seated Liberty design, credited to Christian Gobrecht after a drawing by Thomas Sully, made its appearance on the half dollar in 1839. During that same year the design was modified to include an extra fold of drapery from Liberty's left elbow.

In 1842 the lettering and date were increased in size creating small- and large-date varieties. The 1842-0 small date is a rarity.

The most celebrated rarity of this type is the 1853-0 without arrows and rays of which only three are known to exist.

Arrows at date, reverse rays (1853)

Weight: 12.44 grams. **Composition:** 90-percent silver (.36 ounces), 10-percent copper.

In a move aimed at stopping the disappearance of silver coins from circulation (in the face of rising silver prices) the Mint Act of Feb. 21, 1853, reduced the weight of half dollar from 13.36 grams to 12.44 grams.

As with the other denominations, arrows were added at the date to denote the reduction in weight. In the case of the quarter and half dollar, a glory of rays, emanating from behind the eagle, was also added to the design.

Minted in both Philadelphia and New Orleans, the "arrows and rays" half dollar is a popular one-year type coin.

Reverse rays removed (1854-1855)

James Ross Snowden, who had just entered into service as Mint director, is believed to have ordered the removal of rays in 1854 on the quarter dollar and half dollar, possibly as a means of saving expense on die sinking and die life. [1]

This two-year type was struck at Philadelphia, New Orleans and, in 1855, at San Francisco. Mintage at San Francisco was a low 129,950, making the 1855-S a rare date.

Arrows at date removed (1856-1866)

Although the weight would remain the same, the arrows were dropped from the half dollar design in 1856. This same design was in use at the beginning of the

Civil War and includes coins struck under auspices of the Confederate States of America.

Actually, more than 1.2 million half dollars were struck at the branch mint in New Orleans in early 1861 after Louisiana had officially seceded from the Union and just short of 1 million additional pieces after that state joined the Confederacy. No way is known to readily distinguish the 1861-O coinage as to whether it was struck under the direction of the Union, New Orleans or the Confederacy.

The 1866-S "no motto" strike is scarce in all grades and had a mintage of just 60,000.

Motto above eagle (1866-1873)

Largely through the urging of a Pennsylvania minister by the name of M.R. Watkinson, the motto "In God we Trust" was adopted for use on the quarter, half dollar, dollar, half eagle, eagle, and double eagle in 1866. It had first appeared on the two-cent piece in 1864.

The 1870-CC half dollar is scarce in all grades, with a mintage of 54,617.

Although Mint records indicate that some 5,000 1873-dated coins were struck at the San Francisco Mint prior to the increase in weight, brought on by passage in February of that year of the Coinage Act of 1873, no specimens are known to exist and were likely melted.

Arrows at date (1873-1874)

Weight: 12.5 grams. **Composition:** 90-percent silver (.3618 ounces), 10- percent copper.

Metric conversion was the reason for the increase in weight of the half dollar in 1873 as it had been for the dime and quarter. The half dollar's weight was raised from 12.44 grams to 12.50 grams. Arrows were added at the date to denote the weight increase.

A popular two-year type, the "with arrows" Seated Liberty half dollar was coined at Philadelphia, San Francisco and Carson City. The lowest mintage (59,000) was recorded at the Carson City Mint in 1874.

Arrows at date removed (1875-1891)

Arrows were removed from the date area of the half dollar in 1875, although the weight would remain at the same level. This design would be carried through the remainder of the coinage of Seated Liberty half dollar.

Mintages of the Seated Liberty half dollar were high from 1875 into 1878, when passage of the Bland-Allison Act forced the nation's mints to turn attention to production of the Morgan silver dollar. 1878 would also be the last year of branch-mint coinage of the Seated Liberty half dollar, with just 62,000 struck at Carson City and 12,000 in San Francisco. The latter is especially scarce in all grades.

Mintage at the parent mint in Philadelphia would continue through 1891, but after 1878 at significantly lower levels. Mintage of the half dollar at Philadelphia, which stood at 1.378 million in 1878, plummeted to 5,900 the following year. Through 1890 coinage totals were very low and all dates are scarce in all grades. The last year of coinage of the Seated Liberty half dollar the mintage rebounded to 200,600.

Barber (1892-1915)

Designer: Charles E. Barber. **Size:** 30.6 millimeters. **Weight:** 12.5 grams. **Composition:** 90-percent silver (.3618 ounces), 10-percent copper.

Barber half dollars were struck at four mints including Philadelphia, New Orleans, San Francisco and, beginning in 1906, at the newly established Denver branch mint. Key dates are the 1892-O, 1892-S and the 1897-S.

Walking Liberty (1916-1947)

Designer: Adolph A. Weinman. **Size:** 30.6 millimeters. **Weight:** 12.5 grams. **Composition:** 90-percent silver (.3618 ounces), 10-percent copper.

One of the most popular 20th-century designs (the obverse of which was resurrected beginning in 1986 for the American silver Eagle bullion coin), the Walking Liberty half dollar design was the work of Adolph A. Weinman, who is also credited with designing the Mercury dime.

From 1916 into the following year the mintmark was shown on the obverse. In 1917 it was moved to the reverse, where it was displayed for the remainder of the coinage of the Walking Liberty half dollar.

The 1917-D and 1917-S strikes come in obverse and reverse mintmark varieties. Those with the mintmark on the obverse are scarcer.

Striking was constantly a problem with Walking Liberty half dollar. Several dates are found weakly struck, particularly noticeable on Liberty's left hand as it crosses the body and on head and breast detail of Liberty.

The 1941-S is a leader among notable weakly struck dates in this series. Dates in strong demand, even in the lowest grades, include the 1921, 1921-D, and the 1938-D.

Franklin (1948-1963)

Designer: John R. Sinnock. **Size:** 30.6 millimeters. **Weight:** 12.5 grams. **Composition:** 90-percent silver (.3618 ounces), 10-percent copper.

Statesman, philosopher, and inventor Benjamin Franklin, long a popular subject of medallic art, made his first appearance on a regular-issue U.S. coin in 1948 with the introduction of the Franklin half dollar.

The 1949-S is generally considered the key date in this series, although striking problems with reverse bell lines have proven other dates be much rarer in fully struck condition. Notable in this regard are the San Francisco strikes of 1951-1954 and coinage of the 1960s.

Kennedy (1964 to date)

90-percent silver composition (1964)

Designers: Gilroy Roberts and Frank Gasparro. **Size:** 30.6 millimeters. **Weight:** 12.5 grams. **Composition:** 90-percent silver (.3618 ounces), 10-percent copper.

Following the assassination of President John F. Kennedy, the Mint moved quickly to honor the nation's fallen leader. The Kennedy design by Mint engraver Gilroy Roberts replaced the Franklin design beginning in 1964. The heraldic eagle on the reverse is credited to Frank Gasparro, who later became chief engraver.

Kennedy's popularity made the 1964 date plentiful even in uncirculated, as many of this high-mintage date were saved.

Coinage of the 90-percent silver 1964-dated Kennedy half dollars continued in 1965, with a total mintage in excess of 273.302 million struck at the Philadelphia Mint and an additional 156.205 million coined in Denver, well over any previous coinage of half dollars.

40-percent silver composition (1965-1970)

Weight: 11.5 grams. **Composition:** clad layers of 80-percent silver and 20-percent copper bonded to a core of 79.1-percent copper and 20.9-percent silver (.148 total ounces of silver).

Rising costs of silver and the constant disappearance of the coins from circulation led the Mint to abandon the use of silver in all circulation coins in 1965, with the exception of the half dollar, which continued to be coined in a silver-clad composition. The new composition consisted of an outer shell of 80-percent silver and an inner core of .209-percent silver and .791-percent copper.

The 1970-D silver clad half was available as part of Mint-marketed mint sets and was not released into circulation. The 1965-1969 issues containing 40-percent silver can still sometimes be found in circulation.

Clad composition (1971-1974)

Weight: 11.34 grams. **Composition:** clad layers of 75-percent copper and 25-percent nickel bonded to a pure copper core.

In 1971 the Mint abandoned use of silver in the half dollar and switched to the base-metal clad composition already in use in the dime, quarter and newly released Eisenhower dollar coin.

Bicentennial design, clad composition (1975-1976)

Reverse designer: Seth Huntington.

A design competition, held in honor of the U.S. Bicentennial, open to artists from throughout the country, led to new reverses for the quarter, half dollar and dollar coins struck in 1975 and 1976, but uniformly carrying "1776-1976" dating. Chosen for the half dollar was a design of Independence Hall by Seth Huntington.

Regular design resumed, clad composition (1977 to date)

Regular design resumed, clad composition (1977 to date)

Frank Gasparro's heraldic-eagle reverse returned to the Kennedy half dollar in 1977 and remains in use today. Although largely an unused coinage denomination in today's commerce, suggestions to drop the half dollar from the roster of circulating U.S. coins have yet to come to fruition.

Striking Impressions

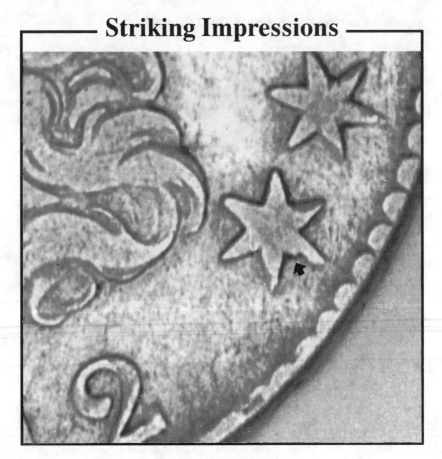

John Reich's 'Scallop'

A notch in the 13th (lower right) star on Capped Bust half dollars dating from 1807 through 1815, 1808 quarter eagles, and certain half eagles was apparently the work of John Reich, mint engraver from 1807 to 1817. Reich, who was criticized for placing his "fat mistress" on his Capped Bust design (introduced in 1807 on the half dollar and half eagle and later used on other denominations), apparently found some reason to mark his obverse dies with a notch on one of the points of the 13th star. Existence of the notches was noted by M.L. Biestle in 1929. Stewart P. Witham, in an article, "John Reich's 'Scallops,'" in the November 1967 issue of *Numismatic Scrapbook Magazine,* further linked the mark directly to Reich, observing that the "scallop" appeared only on Reich's designs and disappeared after Reich left Mint employ in 1817.

— Striking Impressions —

1839 "no drapery"

1839 'no drapery'
Seated Liberty half dollar

In 1839 Christian Gobrecht's Seated Liberty design, which first appeared on the silver dollars of 1836, the quarters of 1837 and the dimes of 1838, was adopted for the half dollar. A die modification, undertaken in early 1839 after the U.S. Mint had begun to produce "no drapery" half dollars, resulted in the addition of an extra fold of drapery extending from Liberty's left elbow to her knee. The "no drapery" 1839 half dollars were released into circulation prior to the change.

Striking Impressions

Scott restrike

Scott token

Confederate half dollar

Following the seizure of the New Orleans Mint by the Confederacy in 1861, plans were implemented by C.G. Memminger, treasury secretary of the Confederate States of America, to produce a Confederate half dollar. Only four proof specimens were struck using the obverse die for the federally issued half dollar of 1861 and a Confederate reverse. The four specimens were presented to dignitaries. The reverse die was later sold, along with one of the specimens, to Philadelphia coin dealer E. Mason Jr., who in turn sold both the coin and die to J.W. Scott & Co. Scott, deciding to strike additional specimens, procured 500 1861-dated half dollars. At first he attempted to overstrike the reverses of 1861 coins with the Confederate reverse die. Finding the results unsatisfactory, he had the reverses of the remaining coins planed off before striking with the Confederate die. Scott also struck 500 white metal tokens using the Confederate reverse die.

Striking Impressions

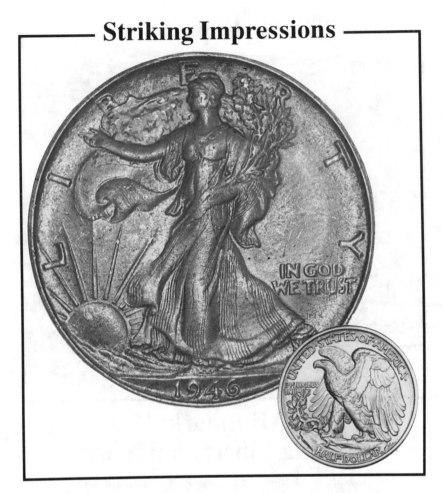

Walking Liberty half dollar

Acknowledged as one of the most graceful designs ever placed on a U.S. coin, Adolph A. Weinman's Walking Liberty half dollar, released in 1916, was a highly symbolic coin. In describing the new coin, the *Report of the Director of the Mint* for 1916 observed that the obverse displayed a full-length figure of Liberty, "the folds of the Stars and Stripes flying to the breeze as a background." It said she is "progressing in full stride toward the dawn of a new day, carrying branches of laurel and oak, symbolical of civil and military glory," with a hand outstretched "in bestowal of the spirit of Liberty." The reverse, the report noted, showed "the eagle perched high upon a mountain crag, his wings unfolded, fearless in spirit and conscious of his power. Springing from a rift in the rock is a sapling of mountain pine, symbolical of America."

Striking Impressions

Mintmark:
Walking Liberty half dollar

Most collectors are familiar with the change in the mintmark positions made early in the coinage of the Walking Liberty half dollar. What is less known is the reason behind the change. When Adolph Weinman's Walking Liberty half dollar was first introduced in 1916 it sported a mintmark just below "In God We Trust" on the obverse of those coins struck in Denver and San Francisco. In 1917, after beginning branch-mint coinage of the 1917-dated half dollars with the mintmark on the obverse, the Mint ordered that the mintmark be moved to the coin's reverse. Mint records show that the change was ordered verbally by Mint Director F.J.H. von Engelken on Feb. 14, 1917. The text of letters held by the Mint, and supplied to *Numismatic News* in 1987, suggest that von Engelken objected to positioning of the mintmark on the coin's obverse simply because he thought it gave the appearance of a defect in the die and was too prominent. The mintmark would remain on the coin's reverse through the end of the series in 1947. The removal of the mintmark during the early part of 1917 created two collectible varieties of that year, with lower mintages on both 1917-D and 1917-S coins with mintmark on obverse.

── Striking Impressions ──

Type I

Type II

Type I/Type II
Franklin half dollar

Beginning with the issues of 1956, a new hub featuring a high-relief eagle was put into use primarily for the production of proof Franklin half dollars. The new hub, however, eventually found its way into use for some circulation-strike Franklins. The Type I hub can be easily distinguished from its high-relief Type II counterpart by counting the number of feathers to the left of the eagle's perch. The Type I design displays four feathers to the left of the perch. The Type II shows only three feathers.

Striking Impressions

Liberty Bell

The Liberty Bell appears on three U.S. coins. It was first used on the reverse of the 1926 Sesquicentennial of American Independence commemorative half dollar (top). Though modeled by John R. Sinnock, credit for the Sesquicentennial half dollar, according to Don Taxay's *An Illustrated History of Commemorative Coinage*, properly belongs to John Frederick Lewis, who made the original sketches. The Liberty Bell was again used on Sinnock's Franklin half dollar design (middle) from 1948-1963. It was most recently displayed overlapping the moon as part of Dennis R. Williams' design for the reverse of the Bicentennial Eisenhower dollar (bottom).

Silver dollars

Flowing Hair (1794-1795)

Designer: Robert Scot. Size: 39-40 millimeters. Weight: 26.96 grams. Composition: 89.24-percent silver (.7737 ounces), 10.76-percent copper.

The nation's first silver dollar was designed by Robert Scot and featured a flowing hair Liberty facing right on the the obverse and a small eagle, perched on a cloud, within a wreath on the reverse.

Mintage of the first-year (1794) issue was a low 1,758, with only around 100 thought to remain in existence.

Most collectors wanting an example of Scot's Flowing Hair dollar will opt for the 1795 issue, with a higher mintage of 160,295. It is, however, also scarce.

Draped Bust (1795-1803)

Small eagle (1795-1798)

Designer: Robert Scot. **Size:** 39-40 millimeters. **Weight:** 26.96 grams. **Composition:** 89.24-percent silver (.7737 ounces), 10.76-percent copper.
Notes: 1798 strikes have either 13 or 15 stars on the obverse.

Modeled after a drawing by portrait artist Gilbert Stuart, the Draped Bust design by Robert Scot was introduced on the dollar in 1795. The reverse continued to portray a small eagle, perched on a cloud, surrounded by a wreath.

Coins struck during this period vary largely in the number and placement of stars. The stars were meant to represent the number of states in the Union.

Mintages of this type were low. Due to its lower weight in comparison to the Spanish and Mexican coins, the U.S. silver dollar was often exported to the West Indies, where it could be exchanged at par for heavier Spanish and Mexican dollars. The foreign coins were then shipped back to the United States to be recoined at the Mint at a profit to the depositor. Early dollars, therefore, rarely reached or remained in circulation.

Heraldic eagle (1798-1803)

Silver dollars continued to be minted through 1803 even though the coins did not circulate and continued to be exported.

It was this design that appeared on arguably the most famous of all U.S. coins, the 1804 silver dollar, termed by collectors "the king of American coins." Although Mint records indicate that some 19,570 1804 silver dollars were struck, research by Eric P. Newman and Kenneth E. Bressett has shown that all of the 15 known specimens were struck much later, the first eight having been minted in 1834 for inclusion in presentation cases to be given to foreign dignitaries.

Restrikes were then made in the late 1850s, one now part of the collection at the Smithsonian Institution, having been struck over a Swiss shooting taler.

Rare proof restrikes of the 1801-1803 dates are also known, having been struck during the late 1850s at the U.S. Mint in Philadelphia.

Gobrecht (1836-1839)

Designer: Christian Gobrecht. **Size:** 38.1 millimeters. **Weight:** 26.73 grams. **Composition:** 90-percent silver (.7736 ounces), 10-percent copper.

The failure of the silver dollar to enter or remain in circulation led President Thomas Jefferson to order a halt to its coinage. It did not resume until 1836 when Christian Gobrecht, a former bank-note engraver, prepared dies based on drawings of a seated Liberty by Thomas Sully and a flying eagle by Titian Peale.

The placement of Gobrecht's name on the obverse die brought criticism and it had to be moved to the base. These first pieces and those dated 1838 are generally considered patterns, while pieces from 1836 with "Gobrecht" on the base of Liberty and those of 1839 are considered to have been struck for circulation.

Unlike the plain-edge 1836 circulation Gobrecht dollars, the 1839 circulation strikes had a reeded edge and show 13 stars around the obverse design and were without stars on the reverse.

Restrikes of the 1836, 1838, and 1839 Gobrecht dollars were made during the late 1850s, and in many cases are rarer than the originals.

Seated Liberty (1840-1873)

No motto (1840-1866)

Designer: Christian Gobrecht. **Size:** 38.1 millimeters. **Weight:** 26.73 grams. **Composition:** 90-percent silver (.7736 ounces), 10-percent copper.

In 1840 full-scale production of silver dollar began again in earnest. Featured was a modeling of Christian Gobrecht's Seated Liberty for the obverse and a heraldic eagle, similar to that already in use on the half dollar and quarter dollar, on the reverse.

The rising price of silver, in the face of burgeoning supplies of gold from California, hindered any chance that silver dollars would circulate. Unlike the half dimes, dimes, quarters and half dollars, which had been reduced in weight to subsidiary level, the silver dollar's weight had not been changed, largely because it represented the unit of value.

The first branch-mint coinage of silver dollars came in 1846 when the New Orleans Mint struck 59,000 Seated Liberty dollars. Rarities include the 1851 and 1852 Philadelphia strikes, with mintages of 1,300 and 1,100, respectively. Restrikes of both of these dates are known in proof.

No dollars were struck for circulation in 1858 and only a small number of proofs were issued.

Motto added on reverse (1866-1873)

In 1866 the addition of the religious motto "In God We Trust" created an additional variety of the Seated Liberty dollar.

This type includes several rare dates, chief among which is the 1870-S, of which fewer than one dozen specimens of an unknown original mintage have surfaced.

Although it is believed that 700 dollars were struck at the San Francisco Mint bearing an 1873 date, no specimens are known to exist.

Also rare are the Carson City dollars of 1871-1873, with mintages of 1,376, 3,150, and 2,300, respectively.

Trade (1873-1885)

Designer: William Barber. **Size:** 38.1 millimeters. **Weight:** 27.22 grams. **Composition:** 90-percent silver (.7878 ounces), 10-percent copper.

The Trade dollar was one of those brilliant ideas that never quite panned out. Proposed as a means of creating a bullion coin that could compete in the markets of the Orient with the popular Spanish and Mexican silver coins, the heavy, 420-grain Trade dollar never really found its market.

Made legal tender in payments up to $5, the Trade dollar soon became a nuisance. The unwanted coins, which found little of the hoped acceptance in the Orient, flooded back into the United States and began to be produced by depositors for domestic circulation.

By 1876 the value of the Trade dollar had fallen to a significant discount below its face value. Under pressure, Congress demonetized the coin in 1876, while allowing its continued mintage for export. Although production for circulation ended in 1878, proofs continued to be struck, in very limited numbers, through 1885.

By the 1880s many of the unwanted, discounted coins had gravitated eastward, where the Trade dollars were often paid out to unsuspecting workers at full face value. In 1887, by which time many of the Trade dollars had fallen into the hands of speculators, the government began redeeming those coins not mutilated, gathering and melting some 7,689,036 pieces. Those pieces that did see circulation in the Far East can be recognized by chopmarks added by merchants who accepted the coins.

Among regular-issue dates, the 1878-CC is a rarity. Although 97,000 were struck, more than 44,000 are known to have been melted by the Mint. The proof-only issues of 1879-1885 are also rare. The 1884, with a mintage of 10, and the 1885, with a mintage of five, are great rarities.

Morgan (1878-1921)

Designer: George T. Morgan. **Size:** 38.1 millimeters. **Weight:** 26.73 grams. **Composition:** 90-percent silver (.7736 ounces), 10-percent copper.

A limited victory was achieved for the forces of free silver with the passage of the Bland-Allison Act of 1878. Free-silver advocates claimed that the elimination of the silver dollar had been surreptitious obtained during congressional passage of the Coinage Act of 1873, which they tagged the "Crime of 1873," and ridiculously blamed for the hardships and depression that followed the Civil War.

Using a fanciful tale of foreign intrigue (centered around a supposed plan by Great Britain to retake control of the Colonies it lost with the Revolutionary War), the free silverites would gain popular and political support running through the presidential election of 1896 in which the cause's greatest champion, William Jennings Bryan, went down in defeat.

The Bland-Allison Act required the Treasury to purchase between $2 million to $4 million is silver ore from domestic producers each month to be turned into silver dollars. Today, because of this vast production of silver dollars, many dates in the Morgan dollar series, including those first produced in 1878, are plentiful. However, subsequent meltings, including nearly 270 million melted as the result of the Pittman Act of 1918, helped to create a number of rarities.

Among the rarest are the 1889-CC, 1893-S and 1894. Of a listed mintage of 12,880 1895 Morgan dollars, only a limited number of proofs exist.

No silver dollars were minted from 1905-1920. Coinage of the Morgan dollar resumed in 1921, the design being replaced in that same year by one marking the restoration of world peace.

Peace (1921-1935)

Designer: Anthony DeFrancisci. **Size:** 38.1 millimeters. **Weight:** 26.73 grams. **Composition:** 90-percent silver (.7736 ounces), 10-percent copper.

World War I was "the war to end all wars" and the Peace dollar, first proposed by noted collector Farran Zerbe, was to be the coin to honor the lasting peace. Designed by Anthony De Francisci and modeled after his wife Teresa, the first-year's issue was struck in high relief, which proved to be impractical for large-scale production, but provided a popular variety for collectors.

The 1928 is considered the key date with the series lowest mintage at 360,649.

Striking Impressions

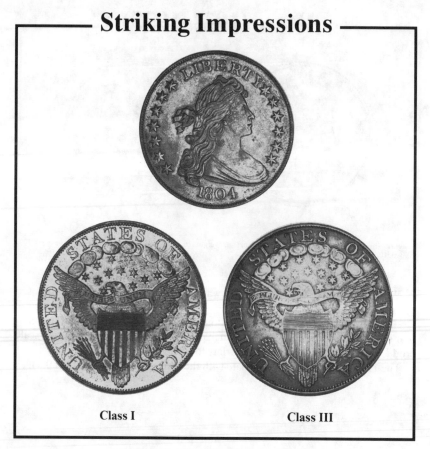

Class I   Class III

1804 silver dollar

The background of the "king of American coins," the 1804 silver dollar, is familiar to most numismatists through the work of Eric P. Newman and Kenneth E. Bressett in their 1963 book, *The Fantastic 1804 Dollar,* Two 1804 silver dollars, of the 15 specimens known, were struck in 1834 as diplomatic gifts for the king of Siam and sultan of Muscat. Specimens were also surreptitiously struck at the Mint in the 1850s and '60s. Bressett and Newman broke the specimens down into three classes based on die positioning and other strike characteristics. The Class I specimens, of which eight examples are known, can be distinguished from the Class II and Class III dollars by the position of "States Of" in "United States Of America" in relation to the clouds on the reverse. For example, the Class I specimens show the "E" in "States" positioned primarily above the fourth cloud from the right. On the Class II (one known) and the Class III specimens, the "E" is between the fourth and fifth clouds from the right. The Class II specimen, struck over an 1857 Swiss Shooting taler, is the only specimen with a plain edge.

— Striking Impressions —

Original

Restrike

Gobrecht dollars

During the late 1850s, the Mint's penchant for accommodating coin collectors led to the creation of restrikes of the 1836-1839 Gobrecht dollars. The easiest method of distiguishing an original Gobrecht dollar, struck in 1836-1839, from one of the restrikes is the die alignment. Though some original Gobrecht dollars used "coin" alignment (reverse inverted when turned) and others "medal" alignment (reverse upright when turned), all show the eagle, on the coin's reverse, flying upward. The restrikes, however, show the eagle in level flight.

Striking Impressions

1870-S
Seated Liberty dollar

The 1870-S silver dollar is a classic rarity of the U.S. coinage series. Only nine or 10 specimens are thought to exist, with one believed to remain in the cornerstone of the old San Francisco Mint building. It has been suggested that the limited mintage may have been created for presentation purposes to mark the laying of the cornerstone of the San Francisco Mint building at Fifth and Mint streets. Known examples bear a small, thin "S" mintmark, located close to the eagle, that is uncharacteristic for the period.

── Striking Impressions ──

Chop marks

The practice of adding "chop marks," or a stamped insignia, to circulating silver coins can be traced to the 18th century. It developed among Oriental merchants as a means of guaranteeing the silver content of coins paid out. Each firm had its own marking and often, after heavy circulation, the design of the host coins would become completely obliterated by chop marks. U.S. Trade dollars, produced from 1873 through 1878 for trade with the Orient, sometimes carry chop marks. The chops indicate that some of the coins did, indeed, circulate in the Far East, despite the consensus that the Trade dollar was largely a failure for the United States.

Striking Impressions

Morgan dollar model

Although she would have preferred to have remained anonymous, two years after the release of the Morgan dollar, a newspaper reporter revealed that the model for George T. Morgan's silver dollar was Philadelphia school teacher Anna Willess Williams. According to an article titled "To Marry A Goddess," appearing in the May 1896 issue of *The Numismatist* (credited to the *New York Mail and Express*), Williams at first resisted modeling for Morgan, but was finally induced by friends to sit for the artist. The article, which also announced Williams' intent to marry, explained that Morgan thought the 18-year-old girl's profile was "the most nearly perfect he had seen in England or America." Williams was further described as a decidely modest young woman who "is slightly below the average height, is rather plump, and is fair. She carries her figure with a stateliness rarely seen and the pose of the head is exactly as seen on the silver dollar. The features of Miss Williams are reproduced as faithfully as in a good photograph." Williams died on April 17, 1926, as the result of a fall in December 1925. *The Numismatist* carried an obituary notice in the May issue, noting Williams was principal of the Girls' School of the House of Refuge in Philadelphia at the time she was recommended to Morgan as model by her former art class instructor Thomas Eakins. The sittings, five in all, were held at Eagans' home in November 1876. According to the May 1926 *Numismatist*, Williams preferred, when questioned, to refer to her modeling simply as "an incident of my youth." The publication was perhaps more gracious in its description of the beauty of the Morgan dollar model than in its prior issue, noting that: "When she became the model Miss Williams' complexion was fair, her eyes blue, her nose Grecian and her hair, which was almost her crowning glory, was of golden color, abundant in quantity and light in texture. It was worn in a becoming soft coil."

Striking Impressions

7 tail feathers

8 tail feathers

7/8 tail feathers

1878 Morgan dollar

Shortly after the release of the first Morgan dollar in 1878, new hubs and dies were created, ostensibly to lower relief, thereby extending die life, and to correct some minor stylistic concerns. One stylistic change concerned the proper number of feathers on the eagle's tail. Previous designs featuring an eagle displayed an odd number of tail feathers. The first 1878 examples show an eagle with eight tail feathers. This was deemed inappropriate, and later strikes show only seven tail feathers. Hubs bearing the seven-tail-feather design were used to overstrike working dies already struck by an eight-tail-feather hub. The result was the popular 1878 7/8 tail feather Morgan dollar variety. A letter from designer George Morgan to Mint Director Henry R. Linderman, published in the *Comprehensive Catalog and Encyclopedia of U.S. Morgan and Peace Dollars*, by Leroy Van Allen and A. George Mallis, reveals that 50 dies were overstruck with the new hub. Coins displaying as few as three to as many as seven of the original eight feathers from beneath the new seven-feather design have been identified.

— Striking Impressions —

Peace dollar model

It was the realization of the childhood dream Teresa De Francisci, wife of the Peace dollar designer Anthony De Francisci, would relate of her use as a model for the silver dollar struck from 1921-1935. In a letter, quoted by Don Taxay in his book *The U.S. Mint and Coinage*, Teresa reminded her brother, Rocco, that she had often posed as Liberty as a child and was heartbroken when she was unable to the play the role in a school play. "I thought of those days often while sitting as a model for Tony's design, and now seeing myself as Miss Liberty on the new coin, it seems like the realization of my fondest childhood dream," she wrote.

Striking Impressions

1964 Peace dollar

A clever mock-up is responsible for the 1964-dated Peace dollar shown above, although the Denver Mint did strike 316,076 coins of that date. Mintage of 45 million silver dollars bearing Anthony De Francisci's design for the 1921-1935 Peace dollar was authorized in August 1964. Production began the following May, but was soon halted. The Treasury, having reconsidered issuance of a coin that critics claimed would benefit only special-interest groups and do little to relieve a coinage shortage, recalled and melted existing specimens. If a specimen or specimens did escape the Mint, as is sometimes rumored, the coin or coins still remain to surface and would likely be subject to confiscation. The fanciful depiction above may, therefore, be as close as any numismatist will ever get to the now legendary 1964 Peace dollar.

Clad dollars

Eisenhower (1971-1978)

Eagle reverse (1971-1974)

Designer: Frank Gasparro. Size: 38.1 millimeters. Weight: 24.59 grams (silver issues) and 22.68 grams (copper-nickel issues). Clad composition: 75-percent copper and 25-percent nickel bonded to a pure copper core. Silver clad composition: clad layers of 80-percent silver and 20-percent copper bonded to a core of 79.1-percent copper and 20.9-percent silver (.3161 total ounces of silver).

Although generally referred to as a "silver dollar," the Eisenhower dollar was the first U.S. dollar to be struck for circulation in base metal. With the exception of special 40-percent silver issues, struck solely for collectors, the entire issue was of a clad composition of copper and nickel.

Designed by Mint chief engraver Frank Gasparro, the coin's obverse honored former President Dwight D. Eisenhower, while the reverse commemorated the first landing on the moon.

Bicentennial design (1975-1976)

Reverse designer: Dennis R. Williams.

The Liberty Bell, superimposed over the moon, as designed by Dennis R. Williams, one of three winners of a Bicentennial design competition to place new reverses on the quarter, half dollar, and dollar, was used on the dual-dated (1776-1976) clad dollars struck in 1975 and 1976.

Regular design resumed (1977-1978)

In 1977 coinage of the Eisenhower dollar continued with Frank Gasparro's original reverse design restored.

Anthony (1979-1981)

Designer: Frank Gasparro. **Size:** 26.5 millimeters. **Weight:** 8.1 grams. **Composition:** clad layers of 75-percent coppe₁ and 25-percent nickel bonded to a pure copper core.

Faced with the continuing problem of the high cost of producing paper money versus it short life span, in 1979 the mint introduced a new mini-dollar that it hoped would gain acceptance in circulation and eventually supplant the paper dollar.

The new dollar coin, which featured suffragette Susan B. Anthony on the obverse and a reduced adaptation of the reverse of the Eisenhower dollar, measured 26.5 millimeters as compared to the former clad dollar of 38.1 millimeters. The new dollar's similarity in size to the quarter dollar led to general distaste by the public for use of the coins.

Mintages were extremely high and the government still holds large quantities.

Striking Impressions

Eisenhower dollar

Designed by Frank Gasparro, the reverse of the Eisenhower dollar used from 1971-1974 and 1977-1978 is closely modeled after the official insignia worn by Apollo 11 astronauts on their historic mission to the moon. It was on July 20, 1969, that Neil Armstrong stepped from the lunar landing module "Eagle" to become the first man to walk on the surface of the moon. The coin's reverse design was replaced in 1975 and 1976 with one showing a Liberty Bell superimposed over the moon in honor of the Bicentennial, but was restored in 1977.

— Striking Impressions —

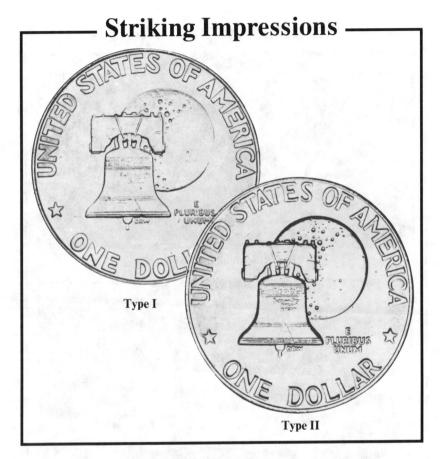

Type I

Type II

1776-1976
Bicentennial dollar

Shortly after the introduction of the Bicentennial dollar, modifications were made to both the obverse and reverse of the coin designs resulting in the creation of two collectible varieties. The relief on the head and base of the portrait of President Dwight D. Eisenhower on the coin's obverse were lowered to allow better metal flow. Details on the Liberty Bell and moon on the coin's reverse were strengthened, while the lettering in "United States of America" and "One Dollar" was narrowed to conform to the obverse lettering. The reverse of the Type I Bicentennial dollar, therefore, displays thicker letters and a tail on the final "S" in "States" that extends up to the middle crossbar of the adjacent "E." The Type II specimen has narrow lettering and the tail on final "S" in "States" extending only slightly above the base of the "E."

— Striking Impressions —

1979 Anthony dollar "near date"

1979 Anthony dollar "far date"

Near- and far-date
1979 Anthony dollars

The 1979 Anthony dollar is known in both near-date and far-date varieties. The first strikes from Philadelphia, and those minted in Denver and San Francisco, show the date farther from the rim. Later that year, Philadelphia would switch to a die with the date nearer the rim, creating the so-called "near date" 1979 Anthony dollar. According to variety specialist Alan Herbert, although some writers cite the width of the rim as a means of distinguishing the near- from far-date varieties, both varieties are known to come with either a narrow or wide rim. The key factor is the distance from the rim.

Striking Impressions

| 1979 Type I | 1979 Type II | 1981 Type I | 1981 Type II |

1979 and 1981
Type I and II mintmarks

The 1979 and 1981 proof coinage offered collectors two types of mintmarks in each year. The worn "S" punch (Type I) used at the beginning of 1979 is often described as resembling a blob, with the "S" being barely recognizable. The new mintmark punch (Type II), introduced later that year and used into 1981, was much better defined. By 1981, however, the new punch (now classified as Type I) had begun to show wear and was replaced by yet another punch (Type II), which was employed through the remainder of the year. The Type II coins of both of these years carry premiums.

Gold dollars

Liberty Head (1849-1854)

Designer: James B. Longacre. **Size:** 13 millimeters. **Weight:** 1.672 grams. **Composition:** 90-percent gold (.0484 ounces), 10-percent copper.

The expression of the basic unit of value in gold did not come until 1849, after the discovery of gold in California. The first gold dollars measured 13 millimeters in diameter, the small size causing a number of problems, including possible confusion with silver coins of roughly the same size and the ease with which the small coins could be lost.

Type 1 gold dollars, as those struck from 1849-1854 have come to be known by collectors, were struck at Philadelphia, Charlotte, Dahlonega, San Francisco and New Orleans mints.

The 1849 coinage is known in both open- and closed-wreath varieties. The 1849-C "open wreath" is a great rarity, with only a handful remaining.

All dates of this type are scarce and mintages were often extremely low, especially at the branch mints. The 1854-D is a key date with just 2,935 minted.

Small Indian Head (1854-1856)

Designer: James B. Longacre. **Size:** 15 millimeters. **Weight:** 1.672 grams. **Composition:** 90-percent gold (.0484 ounces), 10-percent copper.

In 1854 the Type 1 gold dollar was replaced by a larger, thinner gold dollar with the obverse modeled after the $3 gold piece, which began coinage that year. The reverse displayed a wreath of the type that would be use two years later on the Flying Eagle cent.

The Type 2 gold dollar was notorious for its poor striking qualities, noticeable especially at the centers.

Highest mintages of this type came in 1854 and 1855 at the Philadelphia Mint, with 783,943 and 758,269 struck, respectively. Still, all are scarce.

The rarest date is the 1855-D of which only 1,811 were struck. Very few remain in existence. In that same year the New Orleans Mint struck its last gold dollar in a mintage of 55,000.

Large Indian Head (1856-1889)

Designer: James B. Longacre. Size: 15 millimeters. Weight: 1.672 grams. Composition: 90-percent gold (.0484 ounces), 10-percent copper.

Notes: Two varieties of the 1856 strike are distinguished by whether the "5" in the date is slanted or upright. "Closed-3" and "open-3" varieties of the 1873 strike are known and are distinguished by the amount of space between the upper left and lower left serifs in the "3."

Striking problems with the Type 2 gold dollar led to yet another redesign of the gold dollar in 1856. This included lowering the relief and widening the head.

Rarities include the 1856-D (1,460), 1857-D (3,533), 1859-D (4,952), 1860-D (1,566), 1861-D, 1870-S (3,000) and 1875 (420).

The 1861-D was apparently struck after the Confederates States of America had taken over the Dahlonega Mint. Mintage is unknown, although Q. David Bowers estimates that a logical total, when compared to other dates, would be between 1,000-2,000. [1]

Striking Impressions

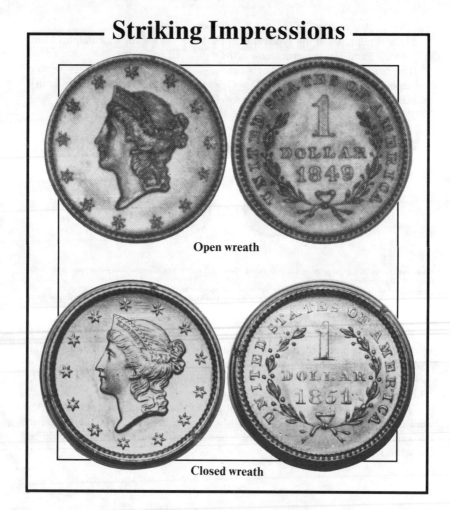

Open wreath

Closed wreath

1849 gold dollar
'Open/closed wreath'

Shortly after the introduction of the nation's first gold dollar in 1849, several modifications were made to James B. Longacre's Type I design. The most obvious change was the closing of the wreath on the coin's reverse. The Philadelphia and Charlotte Mint issues come in both "open wreath" and "closed wreath" varieties, with the 1849-C "open wreath" dollar being of great rarity. The issues of Dahlonega and New Orleans were of the earlier "open wreath" variety only. Variations also exist in the size of the portrait of Liberty on the obverse and the presence or absence of the initial "L" for Longacre.

Gold $2.50

Capped Bust right (1796-1807)

No stars (1796)

Designer: Robert Scot. **Size:** 20 millimeters. **Weight:** 4.37 grams. **Composition:** 91.67-percent gold (.1289 ounces), 8.33-percent copper.
Notes: Varieties of the 1804 strike come with 13 or 14 stars on the reverse.

Robert Scot is credited with the design of the nation's first gold $2.50 piece or quarter eagle. It employed the same obverse as the half eagle introduced the year prior. The reverse of the quarter eagle showed a new heraldic-eagle design, which would later become standard on U.S. gold and silver coins.

This rare one-year type, with a mintage of just 963 coins, lacked stars on the obverse, but did display 16 stars on its reverse. The stars represented the states of the Union, of which Tennessee, the 16th, had been admitted in June of that year.

As with much of the gold series, melting contributed to scarcity of often already low-mintage dates.

Stars (1797-1807)

Shortly after coinage of the first quarter eagle began, the obverse design was changed to include 13 stars, representing the first 13 states. The number of stars on the reverse were dropped from 16 to 13.

Mintage of the quarter eagle was sporadic and total output was low. Estimates of the number of 1796 "with stars" coins struck are placed at 432. The following year's mintage was not much higher, with 427 believed to have been struck.

The highest mintage of the Capped Bust quarter eagle came in 1807, with 6,182 struck. No quarter eagles were minted after 1798 until 1802.

Capped Bust left (1808)

Designer: John Reich. **Sizes:** 20 millimeters (1808), 18.5 millimeters (1821-1827), and 18.2 millimeters (1829-1834). **Weight:** 4.37 grams. **Composition:** 91.67-percent gold (.1289 ounces), 8.33-percent copper.

In 1808 John Reich's portrait of a capped Liberty facing left was placed on the quarter eagle, having been adopted the year prior for the half eagle.

This rare one-year type had a mintage of just 2,710. Coinage of the quarter eagle ended in 1808 and did not resume until 1821.

Capped Head left (1821-1834)

By the time coinage of the quarter eagle began again in 1821, its diameter had been slightly reduced and its design changed to one by Robert Scot.

Mintages were again low, generally between the range of 2,000-6,000 per year. The bottom came in 1826 when only 760 quarter eagles were minted.

The introduction of a closed coinage collar in 1829 further reduced the diameter of the pieces struck thereafter.

Due to meltings, all dates of this design type are rare. A celebrated rarity is the 1834 date with the motto "E Pluribus Unum."

The motto was dropped from the quarter eagle in 1834, when it was redesigned. However, 4,000 quarter eagles were struck of the old design before mintage began of the redesigned quarter eagle. Fewer than one dozen of the 1834 "with motto" quarter eagles are believed to exist.

Classic Head (1834-1839)

Designer: William Kneass. **Size:** 18.2 millimeters. **Weight:** 4.18 grams. **Composition:** 89.92-percent gold (.1209 ounces), 10.08-percent copper.

In 1834 the weight of the quarter eagle and half eagle were lowered. The Liberty design was also remodeled by Mint engraver William Kneass. Gone was the liberty cap and in its place a ribbon, which bound the hair and carried the word "Liberty." Also gone was the motto "E Pluribus Unum."

Mintages of the quarter eagle were much higher than in previous years with even the first-year mintage of 112,234 well exceeding the combined mintage of all prior quarter eagles.

The highest mintage of this type came in 1836 when the Philadelphia Mint churned out 547,986 quarter eagles.

Branch-mint coinage of the quarter eagle would begin in 1838 at the Charlotte Mint. Mintage of this rare date was 7,880. One year later coinage began at Dahlonega and New Orleans.

Coronet Head (1840-1907)

Designer: Christian Gobrecht. **Size:** 18 millimeters. **Weight:** 4.18 grams. **Composition:** 90-percent gold (.121 ounces), 10-percent copper.
Notes: Varieties for 1843 are distinguished by the size of the numerals in the date. "Closed-3" and "open-3" varieties of the 1873 strike are known and are distinguished by the amount of space between the upper left and lower left serifs in the "3" in the date.

In 1840 Christian Gobrecht's Coronet design, which had already come into use on the gold eagle, was placed on the quarter eagle. It would continue to be employed for the next 67 years.

There are several rare dates, including the famous proof-only 1841, of which one dozen are traced; and the 1854-S, with a miniscule mintage of 246 and with less than 10 specimens known to have survived.

In 1848 1,389 quarter eagles were minted bearing a distinctive "Cal." marking above the eagle to show that these coins were struck with gold from California.

Also scarce are a number of the branch-mint issues and later-date Philadelphia quarter eagles.

Among the rare dates are the 1854-S, of which just 243 were struck. Also notable are the low-mintage 1854-1856 Dahlonega quarter eagles and the 1864, 1865, 1875, 1881 and 1885 Philadelphia strikes. The 1863 coinage was in proof only.

Indian Head (1908-1929)

Designer: Bela Lyon Pratt. Size: 18 millimeters. Weight: 4.18 grams. Composition: 90-percent gold (.121 ounces), 10-percent copper.

The last design type for the quarter eagle was also the most unusual. Credited to Bela Lyon Pratt, from an idea of Dr. William Sturgis Bigelow, the new design featured an Indian on the obverse and an eagle on the reverse, both set (along with other design elements) sunken below the field.

However well received artistically, the design brought criticism that coins would not stack properly and that its many crevices would readily attract dirt and possibly help to transmit disease.

Coinage of this type continued uninterrupted from 1908-1915 and then resumed in 1925, running through 1929.

The 1911-D, with this design's lowest mintage (55,680), is the key date.

Striking Impressions

1841
'Little Princess'
proof quarter eagle

Termed by some as the "Little Princess," the 1841 Coronet quarter eagle is one of the great rarities in the quarter eagle series. An enigma in U.S. coinage, there is no known recorded reason for its release and a lack of official mintage figures. Speculation exists that the entire mintage was created in proof for inclusion in presentation sets. Coinage authority Walter Breen records 12 examples in proof, many of which are impaired.

Striking Impressions

1848
'Cal.'
quarter eagle

Sometimes called the first United States commemorative coin, the 1848 quarter eagle with "Cal." stamped on the reverse bears a direct link to the California gold rush. In January 1848 James Marshall discovered gold along a sawmill belonging to his employer, Johann Augustus Sutter. Despite attempts to keep the discovery a secret; news of California's new-found wealth traveled quickly. Less than a year later, California's military governor Col. Richard B. Mason dispatched Lt. Lucien Loeser to Washington, D.C., in August 1848 with samples of California gold. Loeser's samples were subsequently assayed at the Philadelphia Mint, where the gold was transformed into an estimated 1,389 quarter eagles. Each bore a special "Cal." stamp above the eagle as a means of providing special recognition to the source of the gold. Only 50-100 of the 1848 "Cal." quarter eagles are thought to remain in existence, many of which are heavily worn.

Striking Impressions

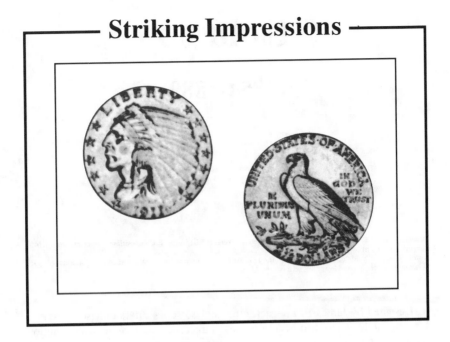

1911-D
Indian Head quarter eagle

The 1911-D is the key date to the Indian Head quarter eagle series with a mintage of 55,680 and as such subject to counterfeiting. Authentication is recommended. Genuine specimens will display a weak mintmark, located to the viewer's left of fasces on the reverse. High-grade specimens also show a wire rim on the obverse between 12 o'clock and 3 o'clock.

Gold $3

(1854-1889)

Designer: James B. Longacre. **Size:** 20.5 millimeters. **Weight:** 5.015 grams. **Composition:** 90-percent gold (.1452 ounces), 10-percent copper.
Notes: "Closed-3" and "open-3" varieties of the 1873 strike are known and are distinguished by the amount of space between the upper left and lower left serifs of the "3" in the date.

Designed by James B. Longacre, the gold $3 series offers only scarce dates. Unfortunately, it has also been a popular target for counterfeiters, and caution must be taken.

The series includes a classic rarity, the 1870-S of which only one is known. A specimen was produced for placement in the cornerstone of what was then the new San Francisco Mint and what now functions as a museum. Whether the one known specimen, formerly part of the Louis Eliasberg collection, is the example intended for the cornerstone of the mint or whether a second specimen resides inside the cornerstone is unknown.

Other rarities include the 1854-D, with a mintage of 6,500 and few survivors, and the 1875 and 1876 proof-only issues.

Striking Impressions

"Closed 3"

"Open 3"

1873
'Closed/Open 3'

Among the more famous coinage varieties, made popular largely through the research of Harry X Boosel, are the 1873 "closed 3" and "open 3." Following the U.S. Mint's preparation and initial use of the coinage dies bearing the 1873 date, chief coiner A. Loudon Snowden complained that the "3" in the date appeared more like an "8." To correct the problem, a new logotype showing an open "3" was introduced on all denominations except the half dime, silver dollar, Trade dollar and gold eagle. In the process, several rarities were created, including the proof 1873 $3 gold piece, which comes in both "closed-3" and "open-3" varieties.

Gold $4

(1879-1880)

Designers: Charles E. Barber (Flowing Hair type) and George T. Morgan (Coiled Hair type).
Notes: These are patterns, rather than coins struck for circulation. Examples in other metals also exist.

Popularity has earned these pattern coins a place in the regular series of U.S. coins. The gold $4 coin or "stella" (after its reverse star), was the brainchild of John A. Kasson, minister to Austria. It was argued that the gold $4, which weighed 7 grams, would fit neatly into a metric system of coinage and would become an internationally accepted coin.

Two versions were issued. One, by Charles Barber, displayed Liberty with flowing hair and the second, by George T. Morgan, showed Liberty with coiled hair. The 1880 Coiled Hair specimen is considered the rarest, with fewer than 10 believed to exist.

Gold $5

Capped Bust (1795-1807)

Small eagle (1795-1798)

Designer: Robert Scot. **Size:** 25 millimeters. **Weight:** 8.75 grams. **Composition:** 91.67-percent gold (.258 ounces), 8.33-percent copper.
Notes: Two 1797 varieties are distinguished by the number of stars on the obverse.

    The gold $5 piece or half eagle holds the distinction of being the first U.S. gold denomination minted, and the only denomination to have been struck at all of the U.S. mints, with the exception of West Point.

    Coinage of the half eagle began in 1795 featuring a depiction of Liberty facing right on the obverse and a small eagle, perched on a olive branch with a wreath in its beak, on the reverse. Ostensibly, the same design would appear on the gold eagle, when coinage began in that same year, and the obverse depiction of Liberty would be used on the gold quarter eagle when it was introduced in 1796.

    Mintages, as with much of the early gold series, were low and survival rates poor. Values are, therefore, very high.

    The 1798 Capped Bust half eagle with small-eagle reverse is a great rarity, with only seven specimens known to exist.

Heraldic eagle (1795-1807)

Notes: 1804 varieties are distinguished by the size of the "8" in the date. 1806 varieties are distinguished by whether the top of the "6" has a serif.

In 1798 the change was made to a heraldic-eagle reverse for the gold half eagle, however, pieces dated 1795 and 1797 with the same reverse are known to exist. These are thought to have been made in 1798, possibly as emergency issues due to constant closings of the Mint because of yellow fever epidemics. [1]

The 1795 and 1797 coinage with heraldic-eagle reverse are great rarities. The 1797 date is represented by specimens with 15 stars on the obverse, of which about a dozen are believed to exist, and by a unique piece showing 16 stars, held in the collection of the Smithsonian Institution.

Many varieties are known and are distinguished by the size of the date punches and the number of stars on the reverse. The 1798, for example, was minted with a 13-star or 14-star reverse.

Overdates are also prevalent. One of the more unusual is the 1802/1, which is of special interest because no half eagles were minted bearing an 1801 date.

Capped draped bust (1807-1812)

Designer: John Reich. **Size:** 25 millimeters. **Weight:** 8.75 grams. **Composition:** 91.67-percent gold (.258 ounces), 8.33-percent copper.
Notes: 1810 varieties are distinguished by the size of the numerals in the date and the size of the "5" in the "5 D." on the reverse. 1811 varieties are distinguished by the size of the "5" in the "5 D." on the reverse.

In 1807 John Reich's design of Liberty, criticized at the time for displaying "the artist's fat mistress," began appearing on the gold half eagle. As with the preceding design, numerous varieties and overdates exist. Rare examples of the 1808 coinage show an 8/7 overdate and the entire mintage of 1809 was struck with a die showing a 9/8.

Capped Head, large diameter (1813-1829)

Notes: 1820 varieties are distinguished by whether the "2" in the date has a curved base or square base, and by the size of the letters in the reverse inscriptions.

Increases in world supplies of silver during this period would make gold the dearer metal and throw the nation's bimetallic system of coinage into havoc. Gold coins disappeared soon after minting and were melted. In the case of the Capped Head half eagle, this led to the melting of large portions of the original mintages and the creation of several highly prized, high-priced rarities.

High on the list are the 1815, with an original mintage of 635 of which a dozen are known to exist; and the famous 1822 half eagle, with an original mintage of 17,796 of which only three examples are known, two being held in the Smithsonian Institution's collection.

The third specimen of the 1822 half eagle, which was formerly part of the Louis Eliasberg collection, sold for $687,500 in auction by Bowers and Ruddy Galleries in 1982.

Other great rarities of this type (to name but a few) include the 1819, all varieties of which are extremely rare; 1825/4, with two specimens known; and the 1829 "large planchet," of which only about a half dozen are known.

Capped Head, reduced diameter (1829-1834)

Notes: 1832 varieties are distinguished by whether the "2" in the date has a curved base or square base and by the number of stars on the reverse. 1834 varieties are distinguished by whether the "4" has a serif at its far right.

The use of the closed coinage collar, beginning in 1829, which confined metal flow as the coin was being struck, made coinage diameters more unified than before and, as in the case of the half eagle, somewhat smaller. Also modified was the date size and other design details, resulting in the creation of the 1829 "small planchet" half eagle, a great rarity, with less than 10 known to exist.

An interesting mistake in 1832 created another rarity in the 1832 "blundered die" variety, showing only 12 obverse stars as compared to the correct 13 stars. Only six specimens of this variety are known.

As with earlier types, most dates are excessively rare, with few surviving of original mintages that ran well over 100,000 per year.

Classic Head (1834-1838)

Designer: William Kneass. **Size:** 22.5 millimeters. **Weight:** 8.36 millimeters. **Composition:** 89.92-percent gold (.2418 ounces), 10.08-percent copper.
Notes: 1834 varieties are distinguished by whether the "4" has a serif at its far right.

Constant melting of gold coins led Congress to lower the weight of all gold denominations in 1834. The weight of the half eagle was dropped from 8.75 grams to 8.36 grams. To readily distinguish the new lower-weight half eagles, the motto "E Pluribus Unum" was removed from above the eagle on the coin's reverse.

Liberty was redesigned by William Kneass, her liberty cap giving way in the new design.

Mintages were much higher than for previous issues with 657,460 struck in the first year alone. The reduced weight also helped keep the coins in circulation and survival rates are much higher.

Branch-mint coinage of the half eagle began in 1838 at the Charlotte (17,179) and Dahlonega (20,583) facilities.

Coronet Head (1839-1908)

No motto (1839-1866)

Designer: Christian Gobrecht. **Size:** 21.6 millimeters. **Weight:** 8.359 grams. **Composition:** 90-percent gold (.242 ounces), 10-percent copper.
Notes: Varieties of the 1842 Philadelphia strikes are distinguished by the size of the letters in the reverse inscriptions. Varieties of the 1842-C and -D strikes are distinguished by the size of the numerals in the date. Varieties of the 1843-O strikes are distinguished by the size of the letters in the reverse inscriptions.

In 1839, following after the redesign of the gold eagle, the half eagle would bear Christian Gobrecht's Coronet head.

This long-lived design continued in use through 1908. Coinage of the Coronet half eagle began at the New Orleans Mint in 1840 and in 1854 in San Francisco.

The 1854-S is a great rarity with a mintage of just 268 and only three specimens known to exist, one of which is in the national coin collection at the Smithsonian Institution.

With motto (1866-1908)

Notes: 1873 "closed-3" and "open-3" varieties are known and are distinguished by the amount of space between the upper left and lower left serifs of the "3" in the date.

In 1866 the motto "In God We Trust" began appearing on the silver denominations above the dime and gold denominations from the half eagle on up.

This type includes coinage from Carson City and Denver, rounding out the seven mints that would strike the half eagle. Survival rates on many of the early dates of this type were low. Rarities include the 1875, with just 200 minted for circulation; and the proof-only 1887 issue, of which only 87 were struck.

Indian Head (1908-1929)

Designer: Bela Lyon Pratt. Size: 21.6 millimeters. Weight: 8.359 grams. Composition: 90-percent gold (.242 ounces), 10-percent copper.

In 1908 Bela Lyon Pratt's Indian Head half eagle was introduced, showing the design detail sunken below the field. The new design was part of a general redesign of the nation's coinage along more artistic lines inspired by President Theodore Roosevelt.

Top rarities in the Indian Head half eagle series include the 1909-0 and 1929.

Gold $10

Capped Bust (1795-1804)

Small eagle (1795-1797)

Designer: Robert Scot. **Size:** 33 millimeters. **Weight:** 17.5 grams. **Composition:** 91.67-percent gold (.5159 ounces), 8.33-percent copper.

Until the introduction of the gold double eagle in 1850, the gold $10 coin or eagle was the highest denomination U.S. gold coin struck. The first pieces, released in very limited mintages from 1795-1797, bore Robert Scot's Capped Bust design on the obverse and his small-eagle design on the reverse. The same design had begun appearing on the half eagle the year prior.

All dates of this type are rare even in low grades.

Heraldic eagle (1797-1804)

Scot's heraldic-eagle reverse was placed on the gold eagle in 1797, having previously appeared on the quarter eagle in 1796.

Constant melting of gold coins (which had become worth more on the bullion market than at face value) led to the suspension of coinage of the eagle in 1804 after some 3,757 coins of that date had been minted.

In 1834 a classic rarity was created when, hoping to assemble diplomatic presentation cases of the nation's coinage, the Mint struck 1804-dated silver dollars and 1804-dated gold eagles. The dollar had not, however, been minted in 1804, coinage having been stopped with the 1803-dated dollar.

The gold eagle had been minted, but the new dies prepared for the 1834 coinage differed from those in use in 1804, including the addition of a beaded border and a different style of "4" in the date.

The 1804 "plain 4," as the 1834 coinage has come to be identified, is a famous rarity in the U.S. series, with only four specimens known to exist, all of which are in proof.

Coronet Head (1838-1907)

No motto (1838-1866)

Designer: Christian Gobrecht. **Size:** 27 millimeters. **Weight:** 16.718 grams. **Composition:** 90-percent gold (.4839 ounces), 10-percent copper.

Coinage of the gold eagle ended in 1804 and did not resume until 1838. During the intervening period most gold coinage was melted.

In 1834 Congress, reacting to the problems associated with the higher price of gold in the face of large supplies of silver, lowered the bullion weight of all gold coins in attempt to keep the coins in circulation.

When coinage of the eagle resumed in 1838 it was at the new lower weight of 16.718 grams as compared to the prior weight of 17.50 grams. Christian Gobrecht's Coronet design replaced the previous design by Robert Scot, and the coin's diameter dropped from 33 millimeters to 27 millimeters.

Branch-mint coinage of the gold eagle began in 1841 at the New Orleans Mint. The scarcest regular-issue date of this type is the 1858, with a mintage of 2,521.

Motto (1866-1907)

Notes: 1873 "closed-3" and "open-3" varieties are known and are distinguished by the amount of space between the upper left and lower left serifs of the "3" in the date.

In 1866 the religious motto "In God We Trust" began appearing on the eagle coinage.

The 1875 is a great rarity with less than 10 of the original mintage of 120 thought to survive.

Indian Head (1907-1933)

No motto (1907-1908)

Designer: Augustus Saint-Gaudens. **Size:** 27 millimeters. **Weight:** 16.718 grams. **Composition:** 90-percent gold (.4839 ounces), 10-percent copper.
Notes: 1907 varieties are distinguished by whether the edge is rolled or wired, and whether the legend "E Pluribus Unum" has periods between each word.

The introduction of the Indian Head eagle was another one of the design changes inspired by President Theodore Roosevelt. An Indian headdress adorns Liberty, modeled by famed sculptor Augustus Saint-Gaudens after a bust originally prepared for the Victory statue in his Sherman monument group in New York. A standing eagle is shown on the coin's reverse.

The 1908 coinage comes in both "no motto" and "motto" varieties, the motto, "In God We Trust," having been added in that year. The experimental pieces of 1907, featuring wire edge or rolled edge, are the great rarities.

Motto (1908-1933)

Protests over the release of so-called "godless" coins led to placement of the motto "In God We Trust" on the gold eagle and double eagle in 1908. The motto had been left off both denominations at Roosevelt's request. Roosevelt is said to have considered the use of the Lord's name on a coin blasphemy.

Rarities include the 1920-S, 1930-S, and 1933. The last of these is a classic rarity, for even though 312,500 1933-dated gold eagles were struck, virtually the entire mintage was melted.

Gold $20

Liberty Head (1849-1907)

"Twenty D.," no motto (1849-1866)

Designer: James B. Longacre. **Size:** 34 millimeters. **Weight:** 33.436 grams. **Composition:** 90-percent gold (.9677 ounces), 10-percent copper.
Notes: In 1861 the reverse was redesigned by Anthony C. Paquet, but it was withdrawn soon after its release. The letters in the inscriptions on the Paquet-reverse variety are taller than on the regular reverse.

In 1848 James Marshall discovered gold on the property of Johann Augustus Sutter in Sacramento, Calif., and the California Gold Rush was on.

The desperate need for gold coins in the West and the influx of supplies of the precious metal led to the introduction of the gold $20 piece, or double eagle, in 1850.

Represented by one example is a pattern 1849-dated double eagle in proof now housed in the national coin collection at the Smithsonian Institution in Washington, D.C. A second specimen is known to have once existed, but its current whereabouts is unknown.

Other rarities include the 1854-O (3,250), 1856-O (2,250), and the 1861 and 1861-S Paquet reverse double eagles. Of the 1861-S Paquet reverse double eagle, Walter Breen traces three specimens known.

"Twenty D.," with motto (1866-1876)

Notes: 1873 "closed-3" and "open-3" varieties are known and are distinguished by the amount of space between the upper left and lower left serif in the "3" in the date.

The motto "In God We Trust" was added to the reverse design beginning in 1866.

The first-year issue of the Carson City Mint, the 1870-CC is a great rarity, with a mintage of 3,789.

"Twenty Dollars" (1877-1907)

Mintages of this third type of Liberty double eagle were high and many dates are relatively common.

Still, there are some scarce, low-mintage dates including the 1879-0 (2,325), 1881 (2,260), 1882 (630), 1885 (828), 1886 (1,106), 1891 (1,442), 1891-CC (5,000) and 1892 (4,523).

In 1883, 1884 and 1887 the Philadelphia Mint struck proofs only.

Saint-Gaudens (1907-1933)

No motto (1907-1908)

Designer: Augustus Saint-Gaudens. **Size:** 34 millimeters. **Weight:** 33.436 grams. **Composition:** 90-percent gold (.9677 ounces), 10-percent copper.
Notes: Lettered-edge varieties have "E Pluribus Unum" on the edge, with stars between the words.

In 1907 one of the most popular coinage designs ever placed on a U.S. coin made its appearance on the double eagle. Designed by noted sculptor Augustus Saint-Gaudens, the obverse showed Liberty striding forward with a torch in her right hand and an olive branch in the left. The reverse displayed a flying eagle.

The first specimens of 1907 struck for circulation were in high relief, with the date shown in Roman numerals. Patterns of that year came in even higher relief, often termed extremely high relief or ultra high relief. Specimens were struck with plain (one known) or lettered edge and are famous rarities.

The high relief, though visually stunning, was found to be impractical for regular coinage. Later issues, including 361,667 struck in 1907, were of lower relief and carried Arabic numerals.

Motto (1908-1933)

As with Augustus Saint-Gaudens' design for the gold eagle, first examples of the double eagle did not include the religious motto "In God We Trust" as part of the design. Protests over the lack of the motto led to its placement on the coin's reverse beginning in 1908.

Rarities include the 1920-S, 1921 and 1927-D. Although 180,000 1927-D double eagles were struck, fewer than one dozen are now believed to exist. Also rare are the dates from 1929-1933.

In 1933 445,500 double eagles were minted in 1933, but none were placed into circulation. A limited number, however, did escape the Mint, and in the past the Treasury has made a case for confiscating examples as being illegal to own.

Striking Impressions

Normal reverse

Paquet reverse

1861 Paquet reverse double eagle

In 1861, Anthony C. Paquet, assistant engraver at the Philadelphia Mint, modified the double eagle's reverse. The most noticeable difference was his use of taller, thinner letters. It was quickly discovered that the new reverse design was wider than the unmodified obverse. The reverse border had become too narrow and would subject the coin to unwanted abrasion. Though the design flaw was discovered quickly, striking of the coins with the modified reverse began at the San Francisco Mint before a message from Mint Director James Ross Snowden halting coinage could arrive. Mint records indicate that 19,250 Paquet-reverse double eagles were struck in San Francisco, though less than 10 examples are known to exist today. Only three specimens of the Philadelphia Mint Paquet-reverse double eagles are thought to exist.

Striking Impressions

Saint-Gaudens
double eagle

The striking beauty of Augustus Saint-Gaudens' high-relief version of the double eagle of 1907 is apparent even in photographs. After issuing 11,250 high-relief specimens for circulation, Mint officials deemed further coinage impractical. The design relief was lowered and Arabic numerals were used for the date in place of Roman numerals on the remainder of the 1907 coinage. Beginning in 1908, the motto "In God We Trust," which had been left off the 1907-dated coins, was placed on the reverse. A small number of ultra-high relief proofs were also struck in 1907.

Striking Impressions

"Plain 4"

"Crosslet 4"

1804
Capped Bust gold eagle

One of the more famous U.S. gold rarities is the 1804 proof eagle with "plain 4" in the date. Despite its 1804 date, this coin was actually struck in 1834 for inclusion in diplomatic presentation cases. Though designated by J. Hewitt Judd, in his *United States Pattern, Experimental and Trial Pieces* as a restrike, the 1804 "plain 4" coins were struck from new dies made specifically for creation of these sets. The 1804 "plain 4" coins also have a beaded border as compared to the denticled border found on the 1804 "crosslet 4" originals. Only four examples of the 1804 "plain 4" are known to exist.

── Striking Impressions ──

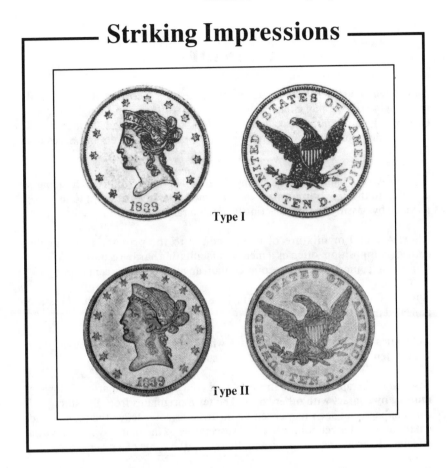

Type I

Type II

Large- and small-letters
1839 eagle

Redesign of Liberty's head in 1839 led to the creation of the so-called large-letters and small-letters 1839 Coronet gold eagle. The Type I 1839 large letters eagle is a carryover of the design from 1838. During 1839 Christian Gobrecht remodeled the Liberty motif for the coin's obverse. The resulting 1839 Type II design showed smaller lettering on the reverse. The large- and small-letter types can be easily distinguished by viewing the coin's obverse. On the Type I 1839 "Head of 1838" coins the point of Liberty's coronet is below the sixth star from the viewer's left. On the Type II coins the coronet point lies more in the center of the space between the sixth and seventh stars. Also, on the Type II coins the date appears centered below the figure of Liberty.

Glossary

Adjustment marks: Marks made by use of a file to correct the weight of overweight coinage planchets prior to striking. Adjusting the weight of planchets was a common practice at the first U.S. Mint in Philadelphia and was often carried out by women hired to weigh planchets and do any necessary filing.

Altered: A coin that has been changed after it left the Mint. Such changes are often to the date or mintmark of a common coin in an attempt to increase its value by passing to an suspecting buyer as a rare date or mint.

Alloy: A metal or mixture of metals added to the primary metal in the coinage composition, often as a means of facilitating hardness during striking. For example, most U.S. silver coins contain an alloy of 10-percent copper.

Anneal: To heat in order to soften. In the minting process planchets are annealed prior to striking.

Authentication: The act of determining whether a coin, medal, token or other related item is a genuine product of the issuing authority.

Bag marks: Scrapes and impairments to a coin's surface imparted following minting by contact with other coins. The term originates from the storage of coins in bags, but such marks can be incurred as coins leave the presses and enter hoppers. Larger coins are more susceptible to the marks, which have an effect on determining the grade and, therefore, the value of a given coin.

Base metal: A metal with low intrinsic value.

Beading: A form of design around the edge of a coin. Beading once served a functional purpose of deterring clipping or shaving parts of the metal by those looking to make a profit and then return the debased coin to circulation.

Blank: Often used in reference to the coinage planchet or disc of metal from which the actual coin is struck. Planchets or blanks are punched out of a sheet of metal by what is known as a blanking press.

Business strike: A coin produced for circulation.

Cast copy: A copy of a coin or medal made by use of a casting process in which molds are used to produced the finished product. Casting imparts a different surface texture to the finished product than striking does and often leaves traces of a seam where the molds came together.

Center dot: A raised dot at the center of coin caused by use of a compass to aid the engraver in the circular positioning of die devices, such as stars, letters and dates. Center dots are prevalent on early U.S. coinage.

Chop mark: A practice used by Oriental merchants as a means of guaranteeing the silver content of coins paid out. The merchants' chop marks, or stamped insignia, often obliterated the original design of the host coin. U.S. Trade dollars, struck for circulation from 1873-1878 and intended for use in trade with China, are sometimes found bearing multiple marks.

Clash marks: Marks left impressed in the coinage dies when the dies come together without a planchet in between. Such marks will affect coins struck subsequently by causing portions of the obverse design to appear in raised form on the reverse, and vice versa, of coins struck following the clash.

Clipping: The practice of shaving or cutting small pieces of metal from a coin in circulation. Clipping was prevalent in Colonial times as a means of surreptitiously extracting precious metal from a coin before placing it back into circulation. The introduction of beading and a raised border helped to alleviate the problem.

Coin alignment: U.S. coins are normally struck with an alignment by which, when a U.S. coin is held by the top and bottom edge and rotated from side-to-side, the reverse will appear upside down.

Collar: A ring-shaped die between which the obverse and reverse coinage dies come during striking. The collar is used to contain the outward flow during striking and can be used to produce edge reeding.

Commemorative: A coin issued to honor a special event or person. In terms of U.S. coinage, commemoratives are generally produced for sale to collectors and are not placed into circulation.

Copy: A replica of an original issue. Copies often vary in quality and metallic composition to the original. Since passage of the Hobby Protection Act (Public Law 93-167) of Nov. 29, 1973, it has been illegal to produce or import copies of coins or other numismatic items that are not clearly and permanently marked with the word "Copy."

Counterfeit: A coin or medal or other numismatic item made fraudulently, either for entry into circulation or for sale to collectors.

Denticles: The toothlike pattern found around the border of a coin.

Die: A cylindrical piece of metal containing an incuse image that imparts a raised image when stamped into a planchet.

Die crack: A crack that develops in a coinage die after extensive usage, defective die, or striking of harder metals. Die cracks, which often run through border lettering, appear as raised lines on the finished coin.

Device: The principal design element.

Double eagle: Name adopted by the Act of March 3, 1849, for the gold coin valued at 20 units or $20.

Eagle: Name adopted by Coinage Act of 1792 for a gold coin valued at 10 units or $10.

Edge: The cylindrical surface of a coin between the two sides. The edge can be plain, reeded, ornamented or lettered.

Electrotype: A copy of a coin, medal or token made by electroplating.

Exerque: The lower segment of coin, below the main design, generally separated by a line and often containing date, designer initials and mintmark.

Face value: The nominal legal-tender value assigned to a given coin by the governing authority.

Fasces: A Roman symbol of authority consisting of bound bundle of rods and an axe.

Field: The flat area of a coin's obverse or reverse, devoid of devices or inscriptions.

Galvano: A reproduction of a proposed design from an artist's original model produced in plaster or other substance and then electroplated with metal. The galvano is then used in a reducing lathe to make a die or hub.

Glory: A heraldic term for stars, rays or other devices placed as if in the sky or as luminous.

Grading: The largely subjective art of providing a numerical or adjectival ranking of the condition of a given coin, token or medal. The grade is often a major determinant of the price of a given numismatic item.

Gresham's Law: The name for the observation made by 16th century English financier Sir Thomas Gresham, that when two coins with same face value but with differing intrinsic value are in circulation at the same time, the one with the lesser intrinsic value will remain in circulation while the other is hoarded.

Half eagle: Name adopted by the Coinage Act of 1792 for a gold coin valued at five units or $5.

Hub: A piece of die steel showing the coinage devices in relief. The hub is used to produce a die which, in contrast, has the relief details incuse. The die is then used to produce the final coin, which looks much the same as the hub. Hubs may be reused to make new dies.

Legend: The principal lettering of a coin generally shown along the coin's outer paremeter.

Lettered edge: Used to describe a coin or medal which has incuse or raised lettering on its edge.

Matte proof: A proof coin in which the surface of the coin has a granular or dull surface. On U.S. coins this type of surface was employed on proofs of the early 20th century. The process has since been abandoned.

Magician's coin: The term sometimes used to describe a coin with two heads or two tails. Such a coin is an impossibility and all are products made outside of the Mint as novelty pieces.

Medal: Made to commemorate an event. Medals differ from coins in that a medal carries no recognized monetary value and, in general, is not produced with the intent of circulating as money.

Medal alignment: Medals are generally struck with the coinage dies facing the same direction during striking. When held by the top and bottom edge and rotated from side-to-side a piece struck in this manner will show both the obverse and reverse right side up.

Mintage: The total number of coins struck during a given time frame, generally one year.

Mintmark: A letter or other marking used on a coin's surface to identify the mint at which the coin originated.

Mule: The combination of two coinage dies not intended for use together.

Numismatics: The science, study or collecting of coins, tokens, medals, paper money and related items.

Obverse: The front or "heads" side of a coin, medal or token.

Overdate: Variety produced when one or more digits of the date are changed at the Mint, generally to save on dies or to correct an error.

Overmintmark: Variety created at the Mint when a different mintmark is punched over an already existing mintmark, generally done to make a coinage die already punched for one mint serviceable at another.

Overstrike: A coin, token or medal produced using a planchet of a previously struck specimen.

Pattern: A proposed coin design issued by the Mint or authorized agent of a governing authority. Patterns can be in a variety of the metals, thicknesses and sizes.

Phrygian cap: A close-fitting, egg-shell shaped hat placed on the head of a freed slave when Rome was in its ascendancy. Hung from a pole, it was a popular symbol of freedom during the French Revolution and in 18th century United States.

Planchet: A disc of metal or other material on which the image of the dies are impressed. Also sometimes called a blank.

Proof: A coin struck twice or more from specially polished dies and polished planchets. Modern proofs are prepared with a mirror finish. Early 20th century proofs were prepared with a matte surface.

Prooflike: A coin that exhibits some of the characteristics of a proof coin, but not all. Many Morgan dollars are found with prooflike surfaces, whereby the field will have a mirror background similar to that of a proof and design details are frosted as some proofs.

Quarter eagle: Name adopted by the Coinage Act of 1792 for a gold coin valued at 2.5 units or $2.50.

Reeding: Serrated (toothlike) ornamentation applied to the coin's edge during striking.

Relief: A design raised above the surface of a coin, medal or token.

Restrike: A coin, medal or token produced from original dies at a later date, often with the purpose of sale to collectors.

Reverse: The backside or "tails" side of a coin, medal or token, opposite from the principal figure of the design or obverse.

Rim: The raised area bordering the edge and surrounding the field.

Series: The complete group of coins of the same denomination and design and representing all issuing mints.

Token: A privately issued piece, generally in metal, with a represent value in trade or offer of service. Tokens are also produced for advertising purposes.

Type coin: A coin from a given series representing the basic design.

Variety: Any coin noticeably different in dies from another of the same design, date and mint.

Wire edge: Created when coinage metal flows between the coinage die and the collar producing a thin flange of coin metal at the outside edge or edges of a coin.

Striking Impressions

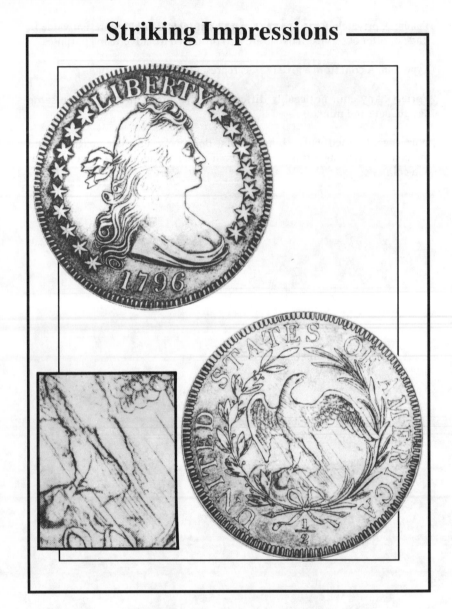

Adjustment marks

During the operations of the first Philadelphia Mint, coin planchets judged to be too heavy were adjusted prior to striking by strokes from a file. To the chagrin of collectors, such adjustment marks were not obliterated by striking and are readily visible on many early U.S. coins.

Striking Impressions

Coinage terms:
Arrows

Arrows were added to the date on the half dimes, dimes, quarters and half dollars of 1853-1855 to denote a reduction in weight and the dimes, quarters and half dollars of 1873-1874 to mark an increase in weight. The changes can be linked to the constantly fluctuating system of bimetallic coinage during the 19th century. The discovery of gold in California in 1849 had a quick impact on the coinage system, setting Gresham's Law into effect as plentiful supplies of gold drove the price of silver up and led to its disappearance from circulation. The Mint Act of 1853 reduced the weight of the half dime, dime, quarter and half dollar in proportional alignment with a 384-grain subsidiary dollar. Arrows were again added in 1873, but this time to signify a slight increase in the weight of the coins to a metric standard.

Striking Impressions

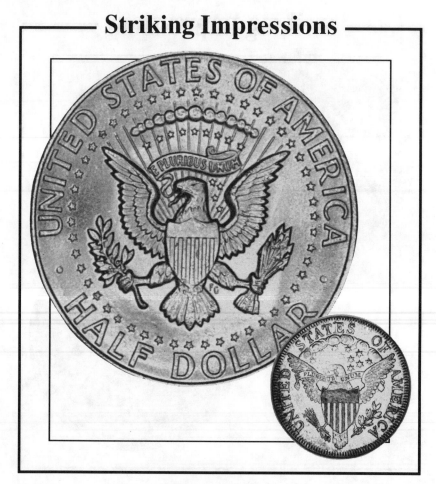

Heraldry:
Arrows and olive branch

Rules of heraldry called for the warlike arrows shown on U.S. coins to be carried in the eagle's sinister (left) claw and the olive branch of peace to be held in the eagle's dexter (right) claw as shown on the enlarged Kennedy half dollar above and all but Robert Scot's first heraldic eagle. When Scot set about preparing the heraldic-eagle reverse found on half dimes (1800-1805), dimes (1798-1807), quarters (1804-1807), half dollars (1801-1807), silver dollars (1798-1803), quarter eagles (1796-1807), half eagles (1795-1807) and eagles (1795-1797), he apparently blundered the proper placement, putting the arrows in the eagle's right claw and the olive branch in the left. Or, perhaps, the placement was intentional act on the part of the young nation in a posturing of strength.

Striking Impressions

Coinage terms:
Bag marks

The term bag mark refers to a nick or cut in the coin's surface that occurs after striking, but before the coin enters circulation. It comes directly from coin-to-coin contact, either in the hoppers at the mint, during bagging or during transport and storage. Larger and heavier coins, such as the silver dollar, were more susceptible to bag marks. Much of the grading of an uncirculated coin is based on the number and severity of bag marks.

Striking Impressions

Coinage terms:
Center dot

One of the less noted aspects of early U.S. coinage production was the use of a center dot as shown on the reverse of this large cent. The dot is the result of the use of a compass to aid the engraver in the circular positioning of letters, stars, dates and other devices on the die.

Striking Impressions

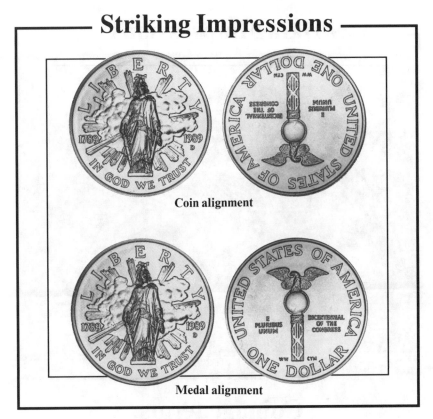

Coin alignment

Medal alignment

Coinage terms:
Coin vs medal alignment

When a U.S. coin is held by the edge between the thumb and forefinger and rotated on its axis from side-to-side, the reverse will be upside down. This relationship is known as "coin alignment." Medal alignment refers to the procedure normally used in striking medals, whereby the coinage dies are both facing the same direction during striking. When turning most medals from side-to-side the reverse will be right side up. The relationship of the dies is generally identified in written descriptions by employing two arrows. In the case of a coin struck with the more normal coin alignment, the first arrow is shown pointing upward and the second downward. In the case of medal alignment both arrows point upward. The relationship becomes important in distinguishing certain 19th-century restrikes struck from original dies but with medal alignment as compared to the originals, which were struck with coin alignment. Not all U.S. coins will display perfect coin alignment, but to have significant value to error collectors such coins should be rotated at least 90 degrees from the normal position.

Striking Impressions

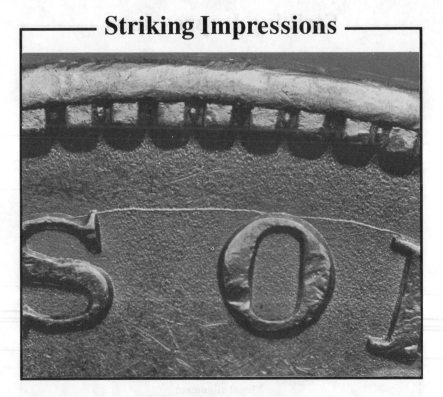

Coinage terms:
Die crack

Die cracking was a constant problem for the U.S. Mint during the 18th and 19th centuries. Once a crack developed in a die, metal would flow into the crack during the striking process, leaving a raised irregular line on the finished coin. Such cracks are often found running through legends and stars along a coin's perimeter. Die cracks are an interesting phenomenon of the minting process and useful to the numismatist in tracing the life of a coinage die, but generally have little or no affect on a coin's value.

Striking Impressions

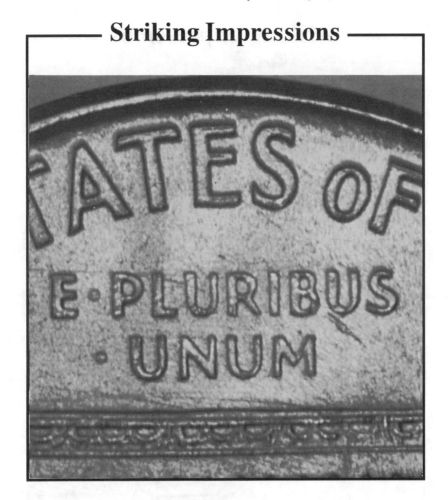

Mottoes:
'E Pluribus Unum'

The motto "E Pluribus Unum," variously translated as "one out of many"; "out of many, one"; "one composed of many"; or "one from many," made its first appearance on a federally issued U.S. coin on the 1796 half eagle with heraldic reverse. Half eagles dated 1795 also bear the motto, but are believed to have been struck in 1798.

—— Striking Impressions ——

Coinage terms: Exergue

A term often seen in coinage descriptions is "exergue." Exergue is defined as the lower circular segment of the coin, generally separated by a line and often containing date, designer initials and mintmark. Examples of its use can be found on such popular coins as the Standing Liberty quarter, Walking Liberty half and Seated Liberty coinage.

── Striking Impressions ──

Fasces

Much of the symbolism on modern coins can be traced to ancient times. The fasces — a bundle of rods bound to a battle axe — was a symbol of authority during the Roman Empire. In the case of the Mercury dime, which shows the fasces entwined by an olive branch, Adolf Weinman, the artist, related that the fasces represented unity of strength; the battle axe, the nation's willingness to defend itself; and the olive branch, this nation's love of peace.

— Striking Impressions —

Heraldry:
Glory

Glory is a heraldic term for stars or rays or other devices placed as if in the sky or as luminous. Many examples exist on U.S. coins, including the 1853 "arrows and rays" half dollar, the Peace dollar, Draped Bust coinage and Barber halves.

Striking Impressions

Mottos:
'In God We Trust'

The motto "In God We Trust" first appeared on U.S. coinage in 1864 on the reverse of the two-cent piece. The idea behind the addition of the religious motto to U.S. coinage is credited to Rev. Mark R. Watkinson, a minister of the First Particular Baptist Church in Ridleyville, Pa. Watkinson wrote to Secretary of the Treasury Salmon P. Chase in 1861 with the suggestion. Various versions of the motto were considered, including "God Our Trust," "Our God and Our Country" and Watkinson's own, "God, Liberty, Law," before the final motto was adopted. The motto now appears on all U.S. coin denominations. In 1955, legislation was passed authorizing its use on U.S. paper money as well.

── Striking Impressions ──

Coinage terms:
Mintmarks

It's sometimes hard to believe that the addition, deletion, alteration or appearance of a tiny, almost imperceptible mark on a coin could cause it to hold or lose substantial value. But that is exactly what can happen. Mintmarks — the minute capital letters found on either the obverse or reverse of most branch-mint coins and recently on most Philadelphia issues — were first used on U.S. coins in 1838. The opening of branch mints in Dahlonega, Ga.; Charlotte, N.C.; and New Orleans presented the need for a ready identification of which mint produced a given coin. Later the branch mints at San Francisco, Carson City, Denver and West Point would be represented by a mintmark. Ironically, although many of the rarest coins are those bearing mintmarks, until the late 19th century coin collectors focused on collecting coins of a given year, paying little or no attention to the existence or lack of a mintmark. It wasn't until A.G. Heaton published *A Treatise on the Coinage of the United States Branch Mints* in 1893 that mintmarks became an important aspect of coin collecting and the value of these small markings began to be appreciated and documented.

Striking Impressions

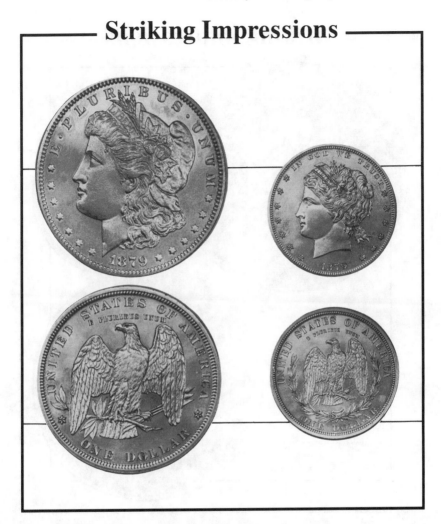

Coinage terms: Mule

A mule is the product of the combination of two coinage dies not normally intended for use together. Exotic examples of mules are plentiful within the U.S. pattern series. During the late 1860s a number of these creations sported either two obverse designs or two reverse designs for the proposed nickel. Shown above, left, is an 1879 dollar mule of the Morgan obverse with a reverse design by William Barber. The reverse is similar to that which appears on the pattern shown at right, and one used on Barber's famous, but unadopted, "Washlady" pattern.

— Striking Impressions —

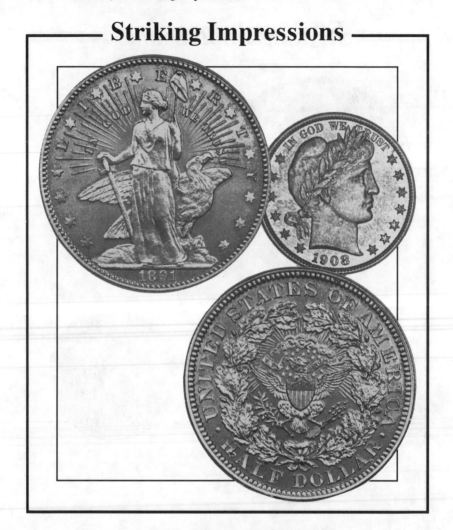

Coinage terms:
Pattern

Before the finished coinage design comes the pattern. Struck in a variety of metals, and often sporting widely different designs than the one finally chosen for use on circulation coinage, patterns represent an interesting collectible field. Rarity and beauty are often key ingredients of the various "might-have-been" coinage designs now sought by collectors. Above is a rare 1891 pattern by Charles E. Barber for the half dollar, showing a standing figure of Columbia, and (at right) the accepted obverse design, employed from 1892-1916 on the dimes and quarters, and from 1892-1915 on the half dollar.

Striking Impressions

Phrygian Cap

Many examples of this ancient symbol of freedom appear on coins of the United States. The Phrygian Cap was a close fitting, egg-shell shaped hat placed on the head of a freed slave when Rome was in its ascendancy. Hung from a pole, it was a popular symbol of freedom during the French Revolution and in 18th-century United States.

Striking Impressions

16 stars   13 stars

Coinage terms: Stars

In 1794 the question of how many stars to place on a U.S. coinage design was easily solved — place 15 stars around the obverse design of the half dime, half dollar, silver dollar to represent the 15 states in the Union. This number included Vermont and Kentucky, which joined the Union in 1791 and 1792, respectively. But the admission of Tennessee as the 16th state on June 1, 1796, cause problems for the Mint and created varieties for collectors of early U.S. coinage. In the half dollar series, for example, the admission of Tennessee led to striking of both 15- and 16-star coins in 1796. By the following year the Mint had determined that continually adding stars to the nation's coinage for each new state was impratical. The solution was to show 13 stars, representing the 13 original states. Again, new varieties were the result. The half dimes of 1797 were struck with 15 stars, 16 stars or 13 stars; the dimes of that year with 16 stars or 13 stars; half eagles with 15 stars or 16 stars; and the dollars of 1798 with 15 stars or 13 stars. Reuse of early coinage dies created some interesting combinations, including a 1799 dollar sporting 13 stars on the obverse and 15 stars on the reverse. By the beginning of the 19th century 13 stars had become the accepted norm, with a few notable exceptions — an 1804 dime and quarter eagle with 13 and 14 stars, an 1817 large cent with 13 stars and 15 stars, the 1836 Gobrecht dollar, and the Kennedy half dollar with 50 stars around the reverse design and an additional 13 stars within the glory emanating from the heraldic eagle.

Endnotes

Half Cents

1. Q. David Bowers, *The History of United States Coinage: As Illustrated by the Garrett Collection* (Los Angeles: Bowers and Ruddy Galleries, 1979), p. 233.
2. Walter Breen, *Walter Breen's Complete Encyclopedia of U.S., and Colonial Coins* (New York: F.C.I. Press, Doubleday, 1988), p. 165.
3. Ibid., p. 171.
4. Ibid. Breen observes that although originally thought to have been minted in proof only, that circulation strikes of the 1831 half cent are known to exist.

Large Cents

1. Don Taxay, *U.S. Mint and Coinage: An Illustrated History from 1776 to the Present* (New York: Arco Publishing Co., 1966) 'p. 104. Taxay quotes from the *Pennsylvania Gazette* of March 20, 1793, of the cent design: "The chain on the reverse is but a bad omen for liberty, and liberty herself appears to be in a fright.-May she not justly cry out in the words of the Apostle 'Alexander the coppersmith hath done me much harm; the Lord reward him according to his works.' The Alexander, Taxay says, is Alexander Hamilton.
2. Breen, *Complete Encyclopedia*, p.188.
3. Taxay, *U.S. Mint and Coinage*, p. 109.

Small cents

1. Breen, *Complete Encyclopedia*, p. 215.
2. Ibid., p. 219. Breen observes that although regular coinage of the oak wreath and shield reverse began in 1860 "many hundreds" of transitional pieces with oak wreath and shield bearing the date 1859 were minted, most in uncirculated, and distributed to dignitaries.
3. Taxay, *U.S. Mint and Coinage*, p. 239-241. Taxay quotes from a letter from Mint Director James Pollock to Secretary of the Treasury Salmon P. Chase arguing against the continued use of the 75-percent copper, 25-percent nickel alloy and in favor a bronze composition already in use in France and England.

Five-cent pieces

1. See Robert R. Van Ryzin, "Which Indian Really Modeled," *Numismatic News*, February 6, 1990, p. 1.

Dimes

1. Walter Breen contends that a portion of the 25,261 mintage listed for 1797 may have been coinage of 1796 delivered in 1797, accounting for the additional rarity of the seemingly higher mintage 1797 coinage. See Breen, *Complete Encyclopedia*, p. 299.
2. Ibid., p. 323.

Quarters

1. Breen, *Complete Encyclopedia,* p. 351.
2. See Robert R. Van Ryzin, "An Artist's Written Word," *Coins* magazine, July 1988, p. 66.
3. See Don Taxay, *U.S. Mint and Coinage,* pp. 360-66, for text of letters and documentation relating to the decision to use Flanagan's design over that of Fraser.

Half dollars

1. Breen, *Complete Encyclopedia,* p. 399.

Gold dollars

1. David Bowers, *United States Gold Coins: An Illustrated History* (Los Angeles: Bowers and Ruddy Galleries, 1982), p. 195.

Gold $5

1. Breen, *Complete Encyclopedia,* p. 515. See also for complete discussion of these issues.

Bibliography

Books:

Attinelli, Emmanuel Joseph. *A Bibliography of American Numismatic Auction Catalogues 1828-1875*. By the author as *Numisgraphics*, 1876; reprint ed. Lawrence, Mass.: Quartermann Publications, 1976.

Breen, Walter. *Walter Breen's Complete Encyclopedia of U.S. and Colonial Coins*. New York: F.C.I. Press, Doubleday, 1988.

Breen, Walter. *Walter Breen's Encyclopedia of United States Half Cents 1793-1857*. Southgate, Calif.: American Institute of Numismatic Research, 1983.

Bowers, Q. David. *The History of United States Coinage As Illustrated by the Garrett Collection*. Los Angeles: Bowers & Ruddy Galleries, 1979.

Bowers, Q. David. *United States Gold Coins: An Illustrated History*. Los Angeles: Bowers & Ruddy Galleries, 1982.

Heaton, A.G. *A Treastise on the Coinage of the United States Branch Mints*. By the author, 1893; reprint ed. New York: Foundation for Numismatic Education, 1984.

Judd, J. Hewitt. *United States Pattern, Experimental and Trial Pieces*. 6th ed. Racine, Wis.: Western Publishing Co., 1977.

Newman, Eric P. and Bressett, Kenneth E. *The Fantastic 1804 Silver Dollar*. Racine, Wis.: Whitman Publishing Co., 1962.

Taxay, Don. *Counterfeit Mis-Struck and Unofficial U.S. Coins*. 4th ed. New York: Arco Publishing Co., 1976.

Taxay, Don. *The U.S. Mint and Coinage: An Illustrated History from 1776 to the Present*. 2nd ed. New York: Arco Publishing Co., 1969.

Taxay, Don. *An Illustrated History of U.S. Commemorative Coinage*. New York: Arco Publishing Co., 1967.

Van Allen, Leroy C. and Mallis, A. George. *Comprehensive Catalog and Encyclopedia of U.S. Morgan and Peace Silver Dollars*. New York: F.C.I. Press, 1976.

Willem, John M. *The United States Trade Dollar: America's Only Unwanted, Unhonored Coin.* New York: By the author, 1959; reprint ed. Racine, Wis.: Western Publishing Co., 1965.

Yeoman, Richard S. *A Guide Book of United States Coins.* Various ed. Racine, Wis. Western Publishing Co.

Journals and magazines:

Dunn, John W. "Design for a Dream Coin." *Coins,* August 1976, pp. 46-49.

"Characteristics of Genuine Key Coins: Cents through Silver Dollars." *The Numismatist* 94 (October 1981): 2718-2720.

"Mr. Weinman Explains Designs on the Coin." *The Numismatist* 29 (December 1916): 544.

Stack's Rare Coin Co. *Coin Review.* Vol. 5, No. 2., 1964.

"To Marry a Goddess: A Young Lady Whose Profile Appears on Uncle Sam's Silver Dollars." *The Numismatist* 9 (May 1896): 101-102.

"The 'Goddess' of Standard Silver Dollar Dead." *The Numismatist* 39 (May 1926): 230-231.

Van Ryzin, Robert R. "An Artist's Written Word: The Letters of Hermon A. MacNeil Bring His Brilliant Career in Sculpture to Life." *Coins,* July 1988, pp. 66-71.

Witham, Stewart P. "John Reich's 'Scallops.' *Numismatic Scrapbook Magazine,* November 1967, pp. 1934-1935.

Newspapers:

Van Ryzin, Robert R. "Which Indian Really Modeled." *Numismatic News,* 6 February 1990, pp. 1, 64-67, 70.

Government documents:

U.S. Congress. Senate. *Coinage Laws of the United States 1792 to 1894 With an Appendix of Statistics Relating to Coins and Currency.* 4th ed. Washington, D.C.: Government Printing Office, 1894.

U.S. Department of Treasury. *Annual Report of the Director of the Mint for the Fiscal Year Ended June 30, 1916 and also Report on the Production of Precious Metals in the Calendar Year 1915.* Treasury Department Doc. 2772. Washington, D.C.: Government Printing Office, 1916.

Silver Value Chart for U.S. and Canadian Coins

Silver Price Per Ounce	$3.00	$3.25	$3.50	$3.75	$4.00	$4.25	$4.50	$4.75	$5.00	$5.25	$5.50	$5.75	$6.00	$6.25	$6.50	$6.75
U.S. 5¢ .350 Fine (Wartime Nickels)	.22	.23	.25	.26	.28	.29	.30	.32	.33	.35	.36	.37	.39	.41	.42	.44
U.S. 50¢ .400 Fine (1965-1970 Clad)	.59	.62	.66	.70	.73	.77	.81	.85	.88	.92	.96	.99	1.04	1.07	1.11	1.15
U.S. $1.00 .400 Fine (Collector Coins)	1.26	1.34	1.42	1.50	1.58	1.66	1.73	1.81	1.89	1.97	2.05	2.13	2.21	2.29	2.37	2.45
U.S. 10¢ .900 Fine (Pre 1965)	.28	.30	.32	.34	.36	.37	.39	.41	.43	.45	.47	.48	.51	.52	.54	.56
U.S. 25¢ .900 Fine (Pre 1965)	.72	.76	.81	.85	.90	.94	.99	1.03	1.08	1.13	1.17	1.22	1.27	1.31	1.36	1.40
U.S. 50¢ .900 Fine (Pre 1965)	1.44	1.53	1.62	1.71	1.80	1.89	1.98	2.07	2.17	2.26	2.35	2.44	2.53	2.62	2.71	2.80
U.S. $1.00 .900 Fine (Pre 1971)	3.09	3.28	3.48	3.67	3.86	4.06	4.25	4.44	4.64	4.83	5.02	5.22	5.41	5.61	5.80	5.99
Canada 10¢ .800 Fine (1920-1967)	.24	.25	.27	.28	.30	.31	.33	.34	.36	.37	.39	.40	.42	.44	.45	.47
Canada 25¢ .800 Fine (1920-1967)	.60	.63	.67	.71	.74	.78	.82	.86	.90	.93	.97	1.01	1.05	1.09	1.13	1.16
Canada 50¢ .800 Fine (1920-1967)	1.20	1.27	1.35	1.42	1.50	1.57	1.65	1.72	1.80	1.87	1.95	2.02	2.10	2.18	2.25	2.33
Canada $1.00 .800 Fine (1936-1967)	2.40	2.55	2.70	2.85	3.00	3.15	3.30	3.45	3.60	3.75	3.90	4.05	4.20	4.35	4.50	4.65
Canada 10¢ .500 Fine (1967 & 1968)*	.15	.15	.16	.17	.18	.19	.20	.21	.22	.23	.24	.25	.26	.27	.28	.29
Canada 25¢ .500 Fine (1967 & 1968)*	.37	.39	.42	.44	.46	.49	.51	.53	.56	.58	.60	.63	.66	.68	.70	.73

Silver Price Per Ounce	$7.00	$7.25	$7.50	$7.75	$8.00	$8.25	$8.50	$8.75	$9.00	$9.25	$9.50	$9.75	$10.00	$10.25	$10.50	$10.75
U.S. 5¢ .350 Fine (Wartime Nickels)	.45	.46	.48	.49	.51	.52	.53	.55	.56	.58	.59	.60	.62	.63	.65	.66
U.S. 50¢ .400 Fine (1965-1970 Clad)	1.18	1.22	1.26	1.29	1.33	1.37	1.40	1.44	1.48	1.52	1.55	1.59	1.63	1.66	1.70	1.74
U.S. $1.00 .400 Fine (Collector Coins)	2.53	2.61	2.69	2.77	2.85	2.93	3.00	3.08	3.16	3.24	3.32	3.40	3.48	3.56	3.64	3.72
U.S. 10¢ .900 Fine (Pre 1965)	.58	.60	.61	.63	.65	.67	.69	.71	.72	.74	.76	.78	.80	.81	.83	.85
U.S. 25¢ .900 Fine (Pre 1965)	1.45	1.49	1.54	1.58	1.63	1.67	1.72	1.76	1.81	1.85	1.90	1.94	1.99	2.03	2.08	2.12
U.S. 50¢ .900 Fine (Pre 1965)	2.89	2.98	3.07	3.16	3.26	3.34	3.44	3.53	3.61	3.71	3.80	3.89	3.98	4.07	4.16	4.25
U.S. $1.00 .900 Fine (Pre 1971)	6.19	6.38	6.57	6.77	6.96	7.15	7.35	7.54	7.73	7.93	8.12	8.31	8.51	8.70	8.89	9.09
Canada 10¢ .800 Fine (1920-1967)	.48	.50	.51	.53	.54	.56	.57	.59	.60	.62	.63	.65	.66	.68	.69	.71
Canada 25¢ .800 Fine (1920-1967)	1.20	1.24	1.28	1.31	1.35	1.39	1.43	1.46	1.50	1.54	1.58	1.61	1.65	1.69	1.73	1.76
Canada 50¢ .800 Fine (1920-1967)	2.40	2.48	2.55	2.63	2.70	2.78	2.85	2.93	3.00	3.08	3.15	3.23	3.30	3.38	3.45	3.53
Canada $1.00 .800 Fine (1935-1967)	4.80	4.95	5.10	5.25	5.40	5.55	5.70	5.85	6.00	6.15	6.30	6.45	6.60	6.75	6.90	7.05
Canada 10¢ .500 Fine (1967 & 1968)*	.30	.31	.32	.33	.34	.35	.36	.37	.38	.38	.39	.40	.41	.42	.43	.44
Canada 25¢ .500 Fine (1967 & 1968)*	.75	.77	.80	.82	.84	.87	.89	.91	.94	.96	.98	1.01	1.03	1.05	1.08	1.10

To figure higher or lower values see back panel.

* The 1967 Canadian 10¢ and 25¢ were produced in both .800 and .500 Fine.

Value Chart for Commonly Traded

Gold Price Per Ounce	$300	$310	$320	$330	$340	$350	$360	$370	$380
USA $1.00 .900 Fine	14.51	15.00	15.48	15.97	16.45	16.93	17.42	17.90	18.38
USA $2.50 .900 Fine	36.28	37.49	38.70	39.90	41.11	42.32	43.53	44.74	45.95
USA $3.00 .900 Fine	43.53	44.98	46.44	47.89	49.34	*50.79	52.24	53.69	55.14
USA $5.00 .900 Fine	72.56	74.98	77.40	79.82	82.24	84.66	87.07	89.49	91.91
USA $10.00 .900 Fine	145.12	149.96	154.80	159.64	164.47	169.31	174.15	178.99	183.82
USA $20.00 .900 Fine	290.25	299.92	309.60	319.27	328.95	338.62	348.30	357.97	367.65
USA Eagle $5.00 .916 Fine	30.00	31.00	32.00	33.00	34.00	35.00	36.00	37.00	38.00
USA Eagle $10.00 .916 Fine	75.00	77.50	80.00	82.50	85.00	87.50	90.00	92.50	95.00
USA Eagle $25.00 .916 Fine	150.00	155.00	160.00	165.00	170.00	175.00	180.00	185.00	190.00
USA Eagle $50.00 .916 Fine	300.00	310.00	320.00	330.00	340.00	350.00	360.00	370.00	380.00
Australia $20.00 .916 Fine	88.42	91.37	94.31	97.26	100.21	103.15	106.10	109.05	112.00
Austria 1 Ducat .986 Fine	33.20	34.31	35.41	36.52	37.63	38.73	39.84	40.95	42.05
Austria 4 Ducat .986 Fine	132.80	137.23	141.65	146.08	150.51	154.93	159.36	163.79	168.21
Austria 10 Francs .900 Fine	28.00	28.94	29.87	30.80	31.74	32.67	33.60	34.54	35.47
Austria 20 Francs .900 Fine	56.01	57.87	59.74	61.61	63.48	65.34	67.21	69.08	70.94
Austria 10 Corona .900 Fine	29.41	30.39	31.37	32.35	33.33	34.31	35.29	36.27	37.25
Austria 20 Corona .900 Fine	58.81	60.77	62.73	64.69	66.65	68.61	70.57	72.53	74.49
Austria 100 Corona .900 Fine	294.06	303.86	313.66	323.46	333.27	343.07	352.87	362.67	372.47
Belgium 20 Francs .900 Fine	56.01	57.87	59.74	61.61	63.48	65.34	67.21	69.08	70.94
Britain ½ Sovereign .916 Fine	35.31	36.49	37.67	38.85	40.02	41.20	42.38	43.55	44.73
Britain 1 Sovereign .916 Fine	70.63	72.98	75.34	77.69	80.05	82.40	84.75	87.11	89.46
Britain 2£ .916 Fine	141.26	145.96	150.67	155.38	160.09	164.80	169.51	174.22	178.92
Britain 5£ .916 Fine	353.14	364.91	376.68	388.45	400.23	412.00	423.77	435.54	447.31
Canada $100 .583 Fine	75.00	77.50	80.00	82.50	85.00	87.50	90.00	92.50	95.00
Canada Maple Leaf .999 Fine	300.00	310.00	320.00	330.00	340.00	350.00	360.00	370.00	380.00
Chile 100 Pesos .900 Fine	176.56	182.45	188.33	194.22	200.10	205.99	211.88	217.76	223.65
Rep China 5 Yuan .999 Fine	15.00	15.50	16.00	16.50	17.00	17.50	18.00	18.50	19.00
Rep China 100 Yuan .999 Fine	300.00	310.00	320.00	330.00	340.00	350.00	360.00	370.00	380.00
Colombia 5 Pesos .916 Fine	70.63	72.98	75.34	77.69	80.05	82.40	84.75	87.11	89.46
France 10 Francs .900 Fine	28.00	28.94	29.87	30.80	31.74	32.67	33.60	34.54	35.47
France 20 Francs .900 Fine	56.01	57.87	59.74	61.61	63.48	65.34	67.21	69.08	70.94
German States 10 Mark .900 Fine	34.57	35.72	36.88	38.03	39.18	40.33	41.48	42.64	43.79
German States 20 Mark .900 Fine	69.14	71.45	73.75	76.06	78.36	80.67	82.97	85.27	87.58
Hong Kong $1000 .916 Fine	141.26	145.96	150.67	155.38	160.09	164.80	169.51	174.22	178.92
Hungary 10 Korona .900 Fine	29.41	30.39	31.37	32.35	33.33	34.31	35.29	36.27	37.25
Hungary 20 Korona .900 Fine	58.81	60.77	62.73	64.69	66.65	68.61	70.57	72.53	74.49
Hungary 100 Korona .900 Fine	294.06	303.86	313.66	323.46	333.27	343.07	352.87	362.67	372.47
Iran 1 Pahlavi .900 Fine	70.31	72.66	75.00	77.35	79.69	82.03	84.38	86.72	89.06
Mexico 2 Pesos .900 Fine	14.46	14.94	15.43	15.91	16.39	16.87	17.35	17.84	18.32
Mexico 2.5 Pesos .900 Fine	18.08	18.68	19.29	19.89	20.49	21.10	21.70	22.30	22.90
Mexico 5 Pesos .900 Fine	36.16	37.37	38.57	39.78	40.99	42.19	43.40	44.60	45.81
Mexico 10 Pesos .900 Fine	72.34	74.75	77.16	79.57	81.98	84.39	86.80	89.21	91.63
Mexico 20 Pesos .900 Fine	144.67	149.50	154.32	159.14	163.96	168.78	173.61	178.43	183.25
Mexico 50 Pesos .900 Fine	361.69	373.75	385.80	397.86	409.92	421.97	434.03	446.08	458.14
Mexico Onza Oro .900 Fine	300.00	310.00	320.00	330.00	340.00	350.00	360.00	370.00	380.00
Netherlands 10 Gulden .900 Fine	58.41	60.36	62.31	64.25	66.20	68.15	70.09	72.04	73.99
Peru 1/5 Libra .916 Fine	14.13	14.60	15.07	15.54	16.01	16.48	16.95	17.42	17.89
Peru 1/2 Libra .916 Fine	35.31	36.49	37.67	38.85	40.02	41.20	42.38	43.55	44.73
Peru 1 Libra .916 Fine	70.63	72.98	75.34	77.69	80.05	82.40	84.75	87.11	89.46
Peru 100 Soles .900 Fine	406.34	419.89	433.43	446.98	460.52	474.07	487.61	501.16	514.70
Russia 5 Roubles .900 Fine	37.34	38.58	39.82	41.07	42.31	43.56	44.80	46.05	47.29
Russia Chervonets .900 Fine	74.67	77.16	79.65	82.14	84.63	87.12	89.61	92.09	94.58
South Africa 1 Rand .916 Fine	35.31	36.49	37.67	38.85	40.02	41.20	42.38	43.55	44.73
South Africa 2 Rands .916 Fine	70.63	72.98	75.34	77.69	80.05	82.40	84.75	87.11	89.46
South Africa Krugerrand .916 Fine	300.00	310.00	320.00	330.00	340.00	350.00	360.00	370.00	380.00
Switzerland 10 Francs .900 Fine	28.00	28.94	29.87	30.80	31.74	32.67	33.60	34.54	35.47
Switzerland 20 Francs .900 Fine	56.01	57.87	59.74	61.61	63.48	65.34	67.21	69.08	70.94
Turkey 100 Piastres .916 Fine	63.81	65.94	68.07	70.19	72.32	74.45	76.57	78.70	80.83

To figure higher or lower values see back panel.

U.S. and World Gold Coins

$390	$400	$410	$420	$430	$440	$450	$460	$470	$480	$490	$500	Change in value per dollar
18.87	19.35	19.84	20.32	20.80	21.29	21.77	22.25	22.74	23.22	23.71	24.19	.0484
47.16	48.37	49.58	50.79	52.00	53.21	54.41	55.62	56.83	58.04	59.25	60.46	.1209
56.59	58.04	59.50	60.95	62.40	63.85	65.30	66.75	68.20	69.65	71.10	72.56	.1451
94.33	96.75	99.17	101.59	104.01	106.42	108.84	111.26	113.68	116.10	118.52	120.94	.2419
188.66	193.50	198.34	203.17	208.01	212.85	217.69	222.52	227.36	232.20	237.04	241.87	.4837
377.32	387.00	396.67	406.35	416.02	425.70	435.37	445.05	454.72	464.40	474.07	483.75	.9675
39.00	40.00	41.00	42.00	43.00	44.00	45.00	46.00	47.00	48.00	49.00	50.00	.1000
97.50	100.00	102.50	105.00	107.50	110.00	112.50	115.00	117.50	120.00	122.50	125.00	.2500
195.00	200.00	205.00	210.00	215.00	220.00	225.00	230.00	235.00	240.00	245.00	250.00	.5000
390.00	400.00	410.00	420.00	430.00	440.00	450.00	460.00	470.00	480.00	490.00	500.00	1.0000
114.94	117.89	120.84	123.78	126.73	129.68	132.63	135.57	138.52	141.74	144.42	147.36	.2948
43.16	44.27	45.37	46.48	47.59	48.69	49.80	50.91	52.01	53.12	54.23	55.33	.1107
172.64	177.07	181.49	185.92	190.35	194.77	199.20	203.63	208.05	212.48	216.91	221.33	.4427
36.40	37.34	38.27	39.21	40.14	41.07	42.01	42.94	43.87	44.81	45.74	46.67	.0933
72.81	74.68	76.54	78.41	80.28	82.14	84.01	85.88	87.75	89.61	91.48	93.35	.1867
38.23	39.21	40.19	41.17	42.15	43.13	44.12	45.10	46.08	47.06	48.04	49.02	.0980
76.46	78.42	80.38	82.34	84.30	86.26	88.22	90.18	92.14	94.10	96.06	98.02	.1960
382.28	392.08	401.88	411.68	421.48	431.29	441.09	450.89	460.69	470.49	480.30	490.10	.9802
72.81	74.68	76.54	78.41	80.28	82.14	84.01	85.88	87.75	89.61	91.48	93.35	.1867
45.91	47.09	48.26	49.44	50.62	51.79	52.97	54.15	55.33	56.50	57.68	58.86	.1177
91.82	94.17	96.53	98.88	101.23	103.59	105.94	108.30	110.65	113.00	115.36	117.71	.2354
183.63	188.34	193.05	197.76	202.47	207.18	211.88	216.59	221.30	226.01	230.72	235.43	.4709
459.08	470.85	482.62	494.40	506.17	517.94	529.71	541.48	553.25	565.02	576.80	588.57	1.1771
97.49	99.99	102.49	104.99	107.49	109.99	112.49	114.99	117.49	119.99	122.49	124.99	.2500
390.00	400.00	410.00	420.00	430.00	440.00	450.00	460.00	470.00	480.00	490.00	500.00	1.0000
229.53	235.42	241.30	247.19	253.07	258.96	264.84	270.73	276.61	282.50	288.39	294.27	.5885
19.50	20.00	20.50	21.00	21.50	22.00	22.50	23.00	23.50	24.00	24.50	25.00	.0500
390.00	400.00	410.00	420.00	430.00	440.00	450.00	460.00	470.00	480.00	490.00	500.00	1.0000
91.82	94.17	96.53	98.88	101.23	103.59	105.94	108.30	110.65	113.00	115.36	117.71	.2355
36.40	37.34	38.27	39.21	40.14	41.07	42.01	42.94	43.87	44.81	45.74	46.67	.0933
72.81	74.68	76.54	78.41	80.28	82.14	84.01	85.88	87.75	89.61	91.48	93.35	.1867
44.94	46.09	47.25	48.40	49.55	50.70	51.86	53.01	54.16	55.31	56.47	57.62	.1152
89.88	92.19	94.49	96.80	99.10	101.41	103.71	106.02	108.32	110.63	112.93	115.24	.2305
183.63	188.34	193.05	197.76	202.47	207.18	211.88	216.59	221.30	226.01	230.72	235.43	.4708
38.23	39.21	40.19	41.17	42.15	43.13	44.12	45.10	46.08	47.06	48.04	49.02	.0980
76.46	78.42	80.38	82.34	84.30	86.26	88.22	90.18	92.14	94.10	96.06	98.02	.1960
382.28	392.08	401.88	411.68	421.48	431.29	441.09	450.89	460.69	470.49	480.30	490.10	.9802
91.41	93.75	96.10	98.44	100.78	103.13	105.47	107.81	110.16	112.50	114.85	117.19	.2354
18.80	19.28	19.76	20.25	20.73	21.21	21.69	22.18	22.66	23.14	23.62	24.10	.0482
23.51	24.11	24.71	25.31	25.92	26.52	27.12	27.73	28.33	28.93	29.53	30.14	.0603
47.01	48.22	49.42	50.63	51.83	53.04	54.25	55.45	56.66	57.86	59.07	60.27	.1205
94.04	96.45	98.86	101.27	103.68	106.09	108.50	110.92	113.33	115.74	118.15	120.56	.2411
188.07	192.90	197.72	202.54	207.36	212.19	217.01	221.83	226.65	231.48	236.30	241.12	.4822
470.20	482.25	494.31	506.37	518.42	530.48	542.53	554.59	566.65	578.70	590.76	602.82	1.2056
390.00	400.00	410.00	420.00	430.00	440.00	450.00	460.00	470.00	480.00	490.00	500.00	1.0000
75.94	77.88	79.83	81.78	83.72	85.67	87.62	89.57	91.51	93.46	95.41	97.35	.1947
18.36	18.83	19.30	19.78	20.25	20.72	21.19	21.66	22.13	22.60	23.07	23.54	.0471
45.91	47.09	48.26	49.44	50.62	51.79	52.97	54.15	55.33	56.50	57.68	58.86	.1177
91.82	94.17	96.53	98.88	101.23	103.59	105.94	108.30	110.65	113.00	115.36	117.71	.2354
528.25	541.79	555.34	568.88	582.43	595.97	609.52	623.06	636.60	650.15	663.69	677.24	1.3544
48.54	49.78	51.03	52.27	53.51	54.76	56.00	57.25	58.49	59.74	60.98	62.23	.1244
97.07	99.56	102.05	104.54	107.03	109.52	112.01	114.50	116.98	119.47	121.96	124.45	.2489
45.91	47.09	48.26	49.44	50.62	51.79	52.97	54.15	55.33	56.50	57.68	58.86	.1177
91.82	94.17	96.53	98.88	101.23	103.59	105.94	108.30	110.65	113.00	115.36	117.71	.2354
390.00	400.00	410.00	420.00	430.00	440.00	450.00	460.00	470.00	480.00	490.00	500.00	1.0000
36.40	37.34	38.27	39.21	40.14	41.07	42.01	42.94	43.87	44.81	45.74	46.67	.0933
72.81	74.68	76.54	78.41	80.28	82.14	84.01	85.88	87.75	89.61	91.48	93.35	.1867
82.95	85.08	87.21	89.34	91.46	93.59	95.72	97.84	99.97	102.10	104.22	106.35	.2127

About the author

Winner of the Numismatic Literary Guild's best all-around portfolio award in national competition in 1989 and 1991, Robert R. Van Ryzin is a longtime collector and past president of local and state numismatic organizations, who turned his love of the hobby into a profession. In 1986 Van Ryzin joined the numismatic editorial staff of Krause Publications in Iola, Wis., after graduating from the University of Wisconsin-Oshkosh with a master's degree in history.

His writings, along with "Striking Impressions," appear regularly in *Numismatic News* and *Coins* magazine.